500 THINGS
you should know about
HISTORY

Andrew Langley
Fiona Macdonald
Jane Walker

Consultant: Richard Tames

TED SMART

This edition produced for
The Book People Ltd, Hall Wood Avenue, Haydock, St Helens WA11 9UL

First published in 2001 by Miles Kelly Publishing Ltd
Bardfield Centre, Great Bardfield, Essex, CM7 4SL

Copyright © Miles Kelly Publishing 2001
This edition printed 2002

2 4 6 8 10 9 7 5 3

Editorial Director: Paula Borton
Art Director: Clare Sleven
Project Editor, Copy Editor: Neil de Cort
Editorial Assistant: Nicola Sail and Simon Nevill
Designer: Sally Lace and Angela Ashton
Artwork Commissioning: Janice Bracken and Lesley Cartlidge
Picture Research: Lesley Cartlidge and Liberty Newton
Proof Reading, Indexing: Lynn Bresler and Jane Parker

ISBN 1-84236-035-3

Printed in Hong Kong

ACKNOWLEDGEMENTS
The Publishers would like to thank the following artists who have
contributed to this book:

Brett Brecon
Chris Buzer/ Studio Galante
Vanessa Card
Brian Dennington/ Allied Artists
Peter Dennis/ Linda Rogers Assoc.
Nicholas Forder
Mike Foster/ Maltings Partnership
Terry Gabbey/ AFA
Luigi Galante/ Studio Galante
Peter Gregory
Brooks Hagan/ Studio Galante
Steve Hibbick/ S.G.A.
Sally Holmes
Richard Hook/ Linden Artists Ltd
Rob Jakeway
John James/Temple Rogers

Andy Lloyd-Jones/ Allied Artists
Kevin Maddison
Janos Marffy
Roger Payne/ Linden Artists Ltd
Terry Riley
Pete Roberts/ Allied Artists
Eric Rowe/ Linden Artists Ltd
Martin Sanders
Peter Sarson
Rob Sheffield
Francesco Spadoni/ Studio Galante
Nick Spender/ Advocate
Roger Stewart
Rudi Vizi
Mike White/ Temple Rogers

Cartoons by Mark Davis at Mackerel

Contents

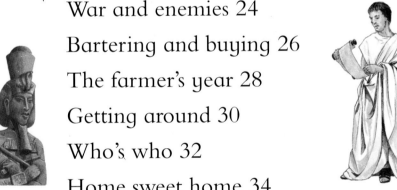

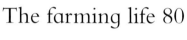

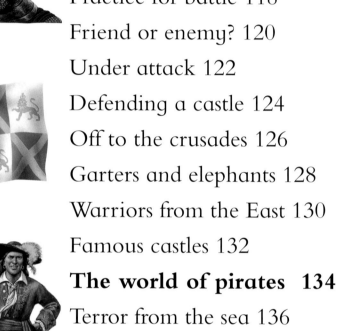
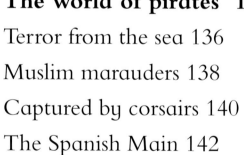

The heart of ancient Egypt

1 **Without the waters of the river Nile, the amazing civilization of ancient Egypt might never have existed.** The Nile provided water for drinking and for watering crops. Every year its floods left a strip of rich dark soil on both sides of the river. Farmers grew their crops in these fertile strips. The Egyptians called their country Kemet, which means 'black land', after this dark soil. The Nile was also important for transport, it was a motorway for the Egyptians!

Royal news

2 **The rulers of ancient Egypt were called pharaohs.** The word 'pharaoh' means great house. The pharaoh was the most important and powerful person in the country. Ordinary people believed he was a god.

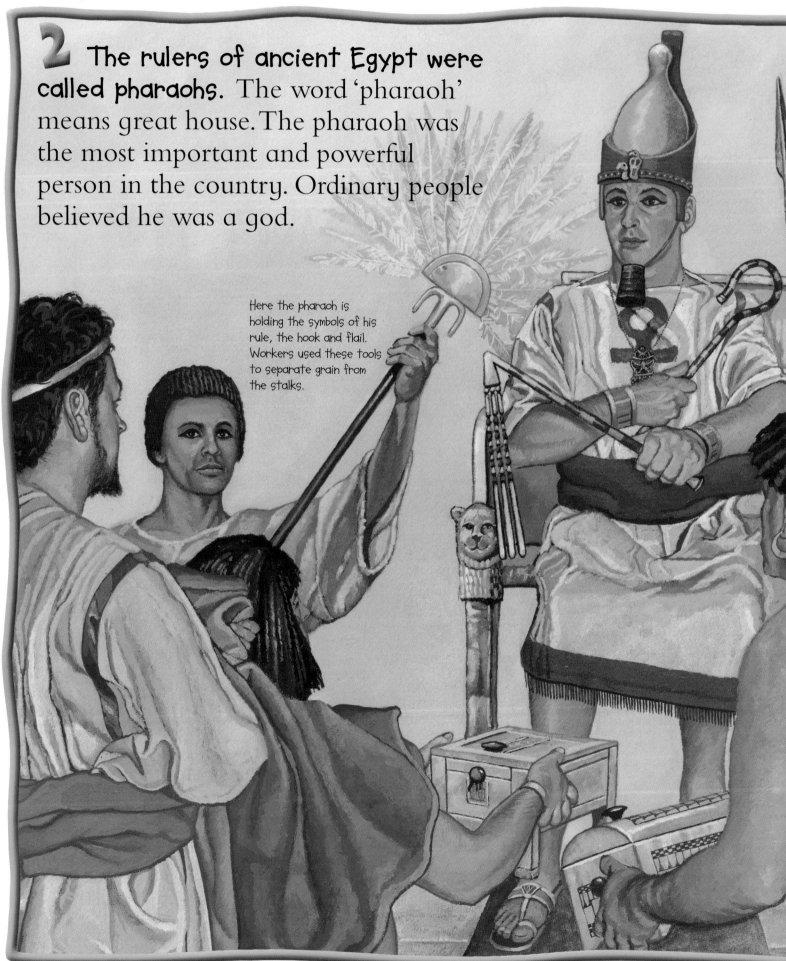

Here the pharaoh is holding the symbols of his rule, the hook and flail. Workers used these tools to separate grain from the stalks.

3 **Ramses II ruled for over 60 years.** He was the only pharaoh to carry the title 'the Great' after his name. Ramses was a great builder and a brave soldier. He was also the father of an incredibly large number of children: 96 boys and 60 girls. Just imagine having 156 brothers and sisters!

These people are paying tribute to the pharaoh. This means that they have come from the surrounding countries to give him presents and tell him how great he is!

4 **The pharaoh often married a close female relative, such as his sister or half-sister.** In this way the blood of the royal family remained pure. The title of 'pharaoh' was usually passed on to the eldest son of the pharaoh's most important wife.

I DON'T BELIEVE IT!

On special occasions, women courtiers wore hair cones made of animal fat scented with spices and herbs. The melting fat trickled down their heads, making their hair sweet smelling – and greasy!

Powerful people

5 Over 30 different dynasties ruled ancient Egypt. A dynasty is a line of rulers from the same family.

6 More than 7,000 years ago, people from central Africa began to arrive in Egypt. They settled in villages along the banks of the Nile and around the Nile Delta. These villages formed the two kingdoms of Upper Egypt (Nile Valley) and Lower Egypt (Nile Delta).

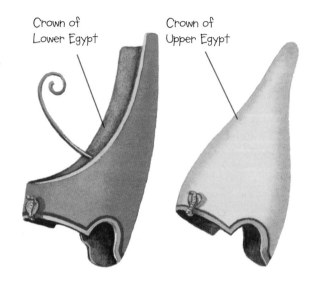

Crown of Lower Egypt

Crown of Upper Egypt

▲ The double crown of Egypt was made up of two crowns, the bucket–shaped red crown of Lower Egypt and the bottle–shaped white crown of Upper Egypt.

▼ This timeline shows the dates of the dynasties of ancient Egypt. The dates are given as a year BC. This means Before Christ. We also say AD, by which we mean After Christ. The year 1 AD is the date from which we start counting the years.

Egypt's first pyramid, the Step Pyramid, was built in 2650 BC.

**2750–2250 BC
OLD KINGDOM
(Dynasties III–VI)**

The Hyksos people invaded in 1670 BC and introduced the chariot.

**2025–1627 BC
MIDDLE KINGDOM
(Dynasties XI–XIII)**

The tomb of the New Kingdom pharaoh Tutankhamun was discovered in 1922.

**1539–1070 BC
NEW KINGDOM
(Dynasties XVIII–XX)**

**3100–2750 BC
EARLY DYNASTIC PERIOD
(Dynasties I and II)**

King Narmer, also called Menes, unites Egypt and records his deeds on what we call the Narmer palette.

**2250–2025 BC
FIRST INTERMEDIATE PERIOD
(Dynasties VII–X)**

As the civilization of Egypt progressed they introduced gods for all different areas of life.

**1648–1539 BC
SECOND INTERMEDIATE PERIOD
(Dynasties XIV–XVII)**

Nilometers were invented to keep track of the height of the river which was very important for the crops.

**1070–653 BC
THIRD INTERMEDIATE PERIOD
(Dynasties XXI–XXV)**

The god Ra was identified at this time with Amun, and became Amun–Ra who was the king of the gods.

7 The history of ancient Egypt began more than 5,000 years ago. The first period was called the Old Kingdom, when the Egyptians built the Great Pyramids. Next came the Middle Kingdom and finally the New Kingdom.

◄ Pharaoh Pepi II (2246–2152 BC), had the longest reign in history – 94 years. He became king when he was only 6 years old.

Queen Cleopatra was the last ruler of the Ptolemaic period.

**332–30 BC
PTOLEMAIC PERIOD**

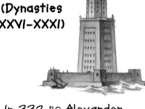

**664–332 BC
LATE PERIOD**
(Dynasties XXVI–XXXI)

In 332 BC Alexander the Great conquered Egypt and founded the famous city of Alexandria.

**30 BC–AD 395
ROMAN PERIOD**

The Roman Emperor Octavian conquered Egypt in 30 BC.

▲ This vizier is checking the sacks of grain that have been brought in from the harvest while a criminal awaits his punishment. The viziers of ancient Egypt were among the most important people in the country.

8 Officials called viziers helped the pharaoh to govern Egypt. Each ruler appointed two viziers – one each for Upper and Lower Egypt. Viziers were powerful men. Each vizier was in charge of a number of royal overseers. Each overseer was responsible for a particular area of government, for example the army or granaries where the grain was stored. The pharaoh, though, was in charge of everyone.

I DON'T BELIEVE IT!
Farmers tried to bribe tax collectors by offering them gifts of goats or ducks in exchange for a smaller tax charge.

Magnificent monuments

9 **The three pyramids at the town of Giza are more than 4,500 years old.** They were built for three kings: Khufu, Khafre and Menkaure. The biggest, the Great Pyramid, took more than 20 years to build. Around 4,000 stonemasons and thousands of other workers were needed to complete the job.

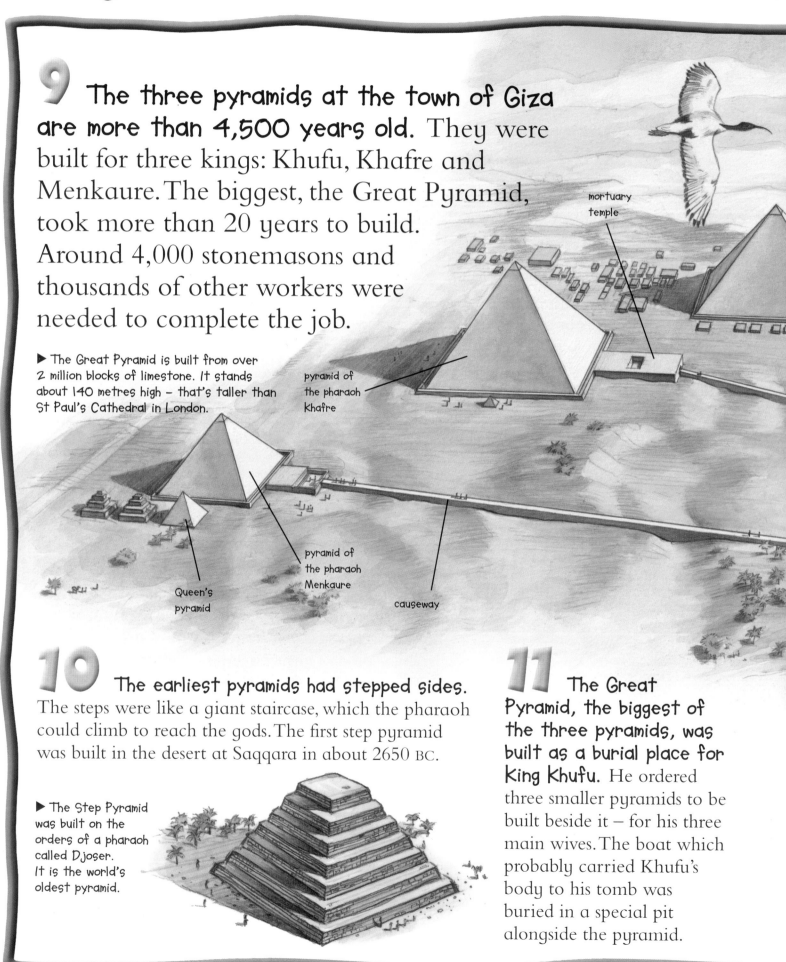

▶ The Great Pyramid is built from over 2 million blocks of limestone. It stands about 140 metres high – that's taller than St Paul's Cathedral in London.

mortuary temple

pyramid of the pharaoh Khafre

pyramid of the pharaoh Menkaure

Queen's pyramid

causeway

10 **The earliest pyramids had stepped sides.** The steps were like a giant staircase, which the pharaoh could climb to reach the gods. The first step pyramid was built in the desert at Saqqara in about 2650 BC.

▶ The Step Pyramid was built on the orders of a pharaoh called Djoser. It is the world's oldest pyramid.

11 **The Great Pyramid, the biggest of the three pyramids, was built as a burial place for King Khufu.** He ordered three smaller pyramids to be built beside it – for his three main wives. The boat which probably carried Khufu's body to his tomb was buried in a special pit alongside the pyramid.

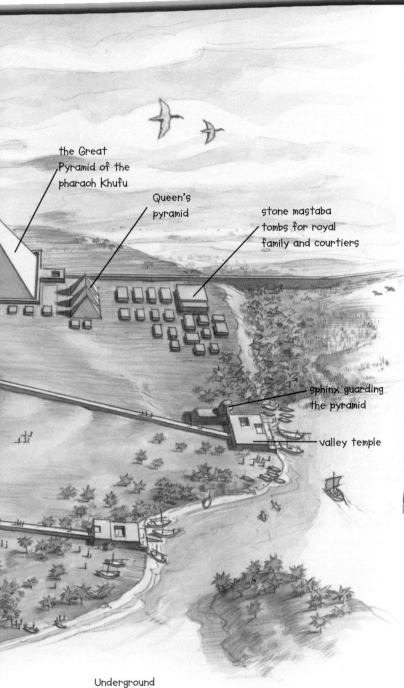

the Great Pyramid of the pharaoh Khufu

Queen's pyramid

stone mastaba tombs for royal family and courtiers

sphinx guarding the pyramid

valley temple

Underground chamber

Pharaoh's Chamber

Grand Gallery

Queen's Chamber

Boat pit

12 The Great Sphinx at Giza guards the way to the Great Pyramid. It is a huge stone statue with the body of a lion and the head of a human. The features on the face were carved to look like the pharaoh Khafre.

I DON'T BELIEVE IT!

A special handbook for tomb robbers called 'The Book of Buried Pearls' gave details of hidden treasures and tips for sneaking past the spirits that guarded the dead!

13 Tomb robbers broke into the pyramids to steal the fabulous treasures inside. To make things difficult for the robbers, pyramid builders added heavy doors of granite and built false corridors inside the pyramids.

14 Inside the Great Pyramid were two large burial rooms, one each for the pharaoh and queen. The Pharaoh's Chamber was reached by a corridor called the Grand Gallery, with a roof more than 8 metres above the floor, four times higher than a normal ceiling. Once the king's body was inside the burial chamber, the entrance was sealed with stone blocks. The last workers had to leave by specially built escape passages.

Supreme beings

15 **The ancient Egyptians worshipped more than 1,000 different gods and goddesses.** The most important god of all was Ra, the sun god. People believed that he was swallowed up each evening by the sky goddess Nut. During the night Ra travelled through the underworld and was born again each morning.

◄ The sun god Ra later became Amun-Ra. He was combined with another god to make a new king of the gods.

16 **A god was often shown as an animal, or as half-human, half-animal.** Below are some of the well-known gods that were represented by animals.

Sobek was a god of the river Nile. Crocodiles were kept in pools next to Sobek's temples.

Bastet was the goddess of cats, musicians and dancers. The cat was a sacred animal in ancient Egypt. When a pet cat died, the body would be wrapped and laid in a cat-shaped coffin before burial in the city's cat cemetery.

The moon god Thoth usually had the head of an ibis, but he was sometimes shown as a baboon. The ancient Egyptians believed that hieroglyphic writing came from Thoth.

Bastet

Sobek

Thoth

17 As god of the dead, Osiris was in charge of the underworld. Ancient Egyptians believed that dead people travelled to the kingdom of the underworld below the Earth. Osiris and his wife Isis were the parents of the god Horus, protector of the pharaoh.

Isis
Osiris
Horus

QUIZ 1

1. Who was buried inside the Great Pyramid?

2. Describe the crown of Upper Egypt.

3. What was a vizier?

4. Which pharaoh ruled for over 90 years?

5. What is the Great Sphinx?

1. King Khufu 2. A bottle-shaped white crown 3. An important governor 4. Pepi II 5. An animal with the body of a lion and the head of a human

18 Anubis was in charge of preparing bodies to be mummified. This work was known as embalming. Because jackals were often found near cemeteries, Anubis, who watched over the dead, was given the form of a jackal. Egyptian priests often wore Anubis masks when preparing mummies.

19 A pharaoh called Amenhotep IV changed his name to Akhenaten, after the sun god Aten. During his reign Akhenaten worshipped only Aten and made Aten the king of all the gods.

Anubis

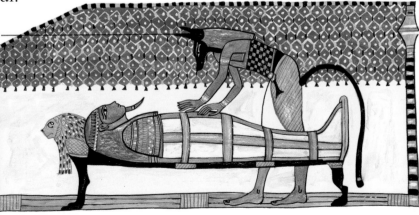

In tombs and temples

20 From about 2150 BC pharaohs were not buried in pyramids, but in tombs in the Valley of the Kings. At that time it was a fairly remote place, surrounded by steep cliffs lying on the west bank of the Nile opposite the city of Thebes. Some of the tombs were cut into the cliffside, others were built deep underground.

▲ Robbers looted everything from the royal tombs – gold, silver, precious stones, furniture, clothing, pots – sometimes they even stole the dead ruler's body!

21 Like the pyramids, the riches in the royal tombs attracted robbers. The entrance to the Valley of the Kings was guarded, but robbers had broken into every tomb except one within 1,000 years. The only one they missed was the tomb of the boy king Tutankhamun, and even this had been partially robbed and re-sealed.

▲ The solid gold death mask of Tutankhamun found in the Valley of the Kings. The young king's tomb was discovered, with its contents untouched, about 80 years ago.

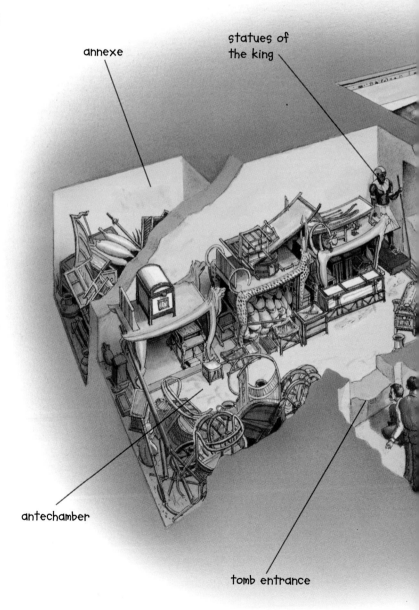

annexe

statues of the king

antechamber

tomb entrance

22 Archaeologist Howard Carter discovered the tomb of Tutankhamun in 1922. An archaeologist is someone who searches for historical objects. Tutankhamun's body was found inside a nest of three mummy cases in a sarcophagus (stone coffin). The sarcophagus was inside a set of four wooden shrines big enough to contain a modern car.

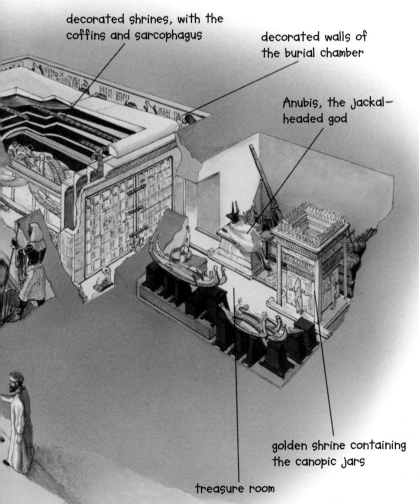

decorated shrines, with the coffins and sarcophagus

decorated walls of the burial chamber

Anubis, the jackal-headed god

golden shrine containing the canopic jars

treasure room

Carter, and his sponsor Lord Carnarvon, finally found Tutankhamun's tomb after five years of archaeological exploration in Egypt. Carnarvon died just 4 months after he first entered the tomb. Some people said he was the victim of Tutankhamun's 'curse' because he had disturbed the pharaoh's body. In fact Carnarvon died from an infected mosquito bite.

23 The ancient Egyptians built fabulous temples to worship their gods. Powerful priests ruled over the temples, and the riches and lands attached to them. Many of the finest temples were dedicated to Amun-Ra, king of the gods.

24 The temple at Abu Simbel, in the south of Egypt, is carved out of sandstone rock. It was built on the orders of Ramses II. The temple was built in such a way that on two days each year (February 22 and October 22) the Sun's first rays shine on the back of the inner room, lighting up statues of the gods.

▲ Four enormous statues of Ramses II, each over 20 metres high, guard the temple entrance at Abu Simbel.

Big building blocks!

25 Each block used to build the Great Pyramid weighed as much as two and a half adult elephants! Labourers used copper chisels and saws to cut and shape the stones before dragging them on wooden sledges to the base of the pyramid.

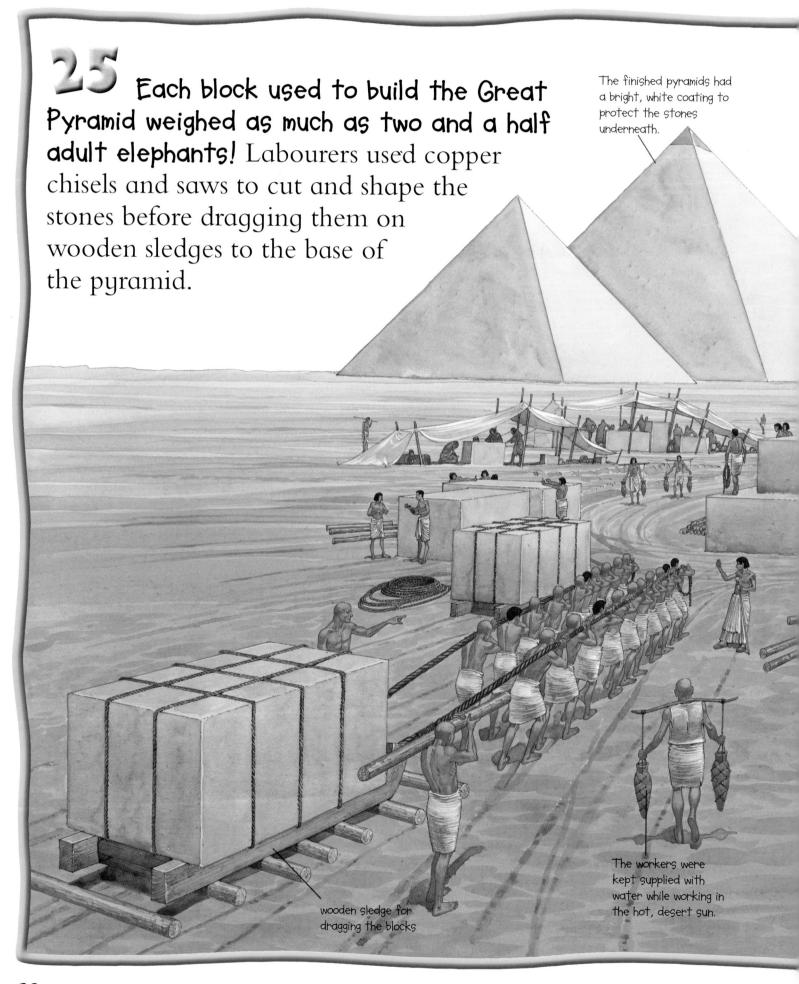

The finished pyramids had a bright, white coating to protect the stones underneath.

wooden sledge for dragging the blocks

The workers were kept supplied with water while working in the hot, desert sun.

The huge stones had to be levered into exactly the right position.

Up to two million of these blocks could be used to make one pyramid. It could take as long as 20 years.

Teams of workers had to drag the stones up the slopes.

Some people now think that the stones were levered into place, not pulled up a slope.

26 Steep ramps of earth and mud brick were built to raise the stones onto the pyramid structure. As each new layer of stones was laid in position, the ramps were lengthened to allow workers to build the next layer.

I DON'T BELIEVE IT!

Imhotep, the architect of the Step Pyramid at Saqqara, was a busy man – he was also a vizier, a doctor, a scribe, a high priest and a poet! He served under a total of four different kings.

Making mummies

27 Making a mummy was difficult and skilled work. First the brain, stomach, lungs and other organs were removed, but the heart was left in place. Next, the body was covered with salts and left to dry for up to 40 days. The dried body was washed and filled with linen and other stuffing to keep its shape. Finally, it was oiled and wrapped in layers of linen bandages.

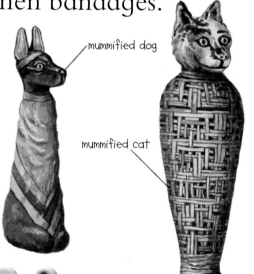

mummified dog

mummified cat

The priest in charge wore a jackal mask to represent the god Anubis.

The organs were stored in canopic jars like these. Each jar represented a god.

amulet placed with the mummy for luck

28 Animals were made into mummies too. A nobleman might be buried with a mummy of his pet cat. Mummification was expensive, so people only preserved animals in this way to offer them to the gods. One mummified crocodile discovered by archaeologists was over 4.5 metres long!

29 Body parts were removed from the dead person and stored in special containers. The stomach, intestines, lungs and liver were cut out and stored in four separate jars, called canopic jars.

wooden coffin for the body

MAKE A DEATH MASK

You will need

a play mask (made of plastic or stiff card)
PVA glue   a paintbrush
newspaper   poster paints
white paint

Use an inexpensive play mask, such as a Halloween one, as your basic mask. Cover the mask with a thick layer of PVA glue. Spread layers of torn newspaper strips over the mask and leave to dry.

Cover the mask with white paint. When dry, use the poster paints to create an amazing death mask of your own! If you haven't got gold-coloured paint, you can use gold glitter to create the same effect.

30 A mask was fitted over the face of a mummy. The ancient Egyptians believed that the mask would help the dead person's spirit to recognize the mummy later on. A pharaoh's mummy mask was made of gold and precious stones.

31 When ready for burial, a mummy was placed inside a special case. Some cases were simple wooden boxes, but others were shaped like mummies and richly decorated. The mummy case of an important person, such as a pharaoh or a nobleman, was sealed inside a stone coffin called a sarcophagus.

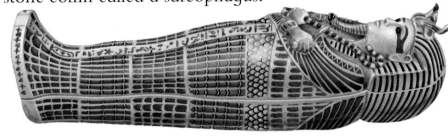

War and enemies

32 Foot soldiers carried metal swords and spears, with shields made of wood or ox hide. Later, soldiers were protected by body armour made from strips of leather.

▲ During the New Kingdom, Egypt created a professional army of trained soldiers. Soldiers had strong shields and a long and deadly spear.

33 Specially trained soldiers fired arrows from their bows while riding in horse-drawn chariots. Each chariot carried two soldiers and was pulled by a pair of horses. During the time of the New Kingdom (around 3,500 years ago), this new kind of war weapon helped the Egyptians to defeat several invading armies.

▲ The Egyptians were gradually taken over by the Hyksos people from the east. The Hyksos introduced the horse-drawn chariot into Egypt. The Egyptians copied the chariot and eventually used it to defeat the Hyksos and drive them out.

34 The Sea People attacked Egypt during the reign of Ramses III.
These raiders came from the northeastern corner of the Mediterranean. Ramses sent a fleet of warships to defeat them.

▼ Ramses III fought off three separate lots of invaders, including the Sea People. Warships were used by Ramses to defeat the Sea People.

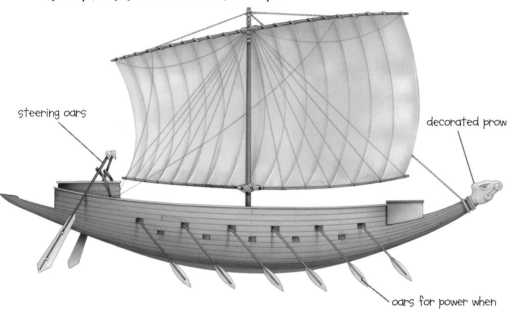

steering oars

decorated prow

oars for power when there was no wind

35 A general called Ptolemy won control of Egypt in 323 BC.
He was the first of several rulers who made up the Ptolemaic dynasty. Under the Ptolemies, the city of Alexandria, on the Mediterranean Sea, became the new Egyptian capital and an important city for art and culture.

fires kept burning to warn ships

▶ The great harbours at Alexandria were guarded by the huge Pharos, the first lighthouse in the world (and one of the Seven Wonders of the Ancient World). The city also had a museum and a vast library containing up to 500,000 books.

▼ The Hyksos invaders conquered Lower Egypt during the 1700s BC. They did not reach Thebes, but made their capital at Avaris.

Sea People
Tarsus
Antioch
MEDITERRANEAN SEA
Hyksos
Jerusalem
Alexandria
Tanis
Avaris
Memphis
Thebes
Abu Simbel

36 The Hyksos people conquered Egypt in about 1700 BC.
They ruled the Egyptians for 200 years. They introduced the horse, the chariot and other new weapons which the Egyptians eventually used to conquer an empire.

I DON'T BELIEVE IT!
Soldiers who fought bravely in battle were awarded golden fly medals – for 'buzzing' the enemy so successfully!

25

Bartering and buying

37 Egyptian traders did not use money to buy and sell goods. Instead they bartered (exchanged goods) with other traders. Merchants visited the countries bordering the Mediterranean Sea as well as those lands to the south. The Egyptians offered goods such as gold, a kind of paper called papyrus, and cattle.

▲ These Egyptian workers are carrying their oil to market. When they arrive, they can exchange their oil for anything they need, such as food or clothes.

38 Merchants brought back exotic goods from the land of Nubia, to the south of Egypt. These included leopard skins, elephant tusks, ostrich feathers – and slaves. One of the main trading posts where goods were exchanged was the town of Kerma, on the river Nile beyond Egypt.

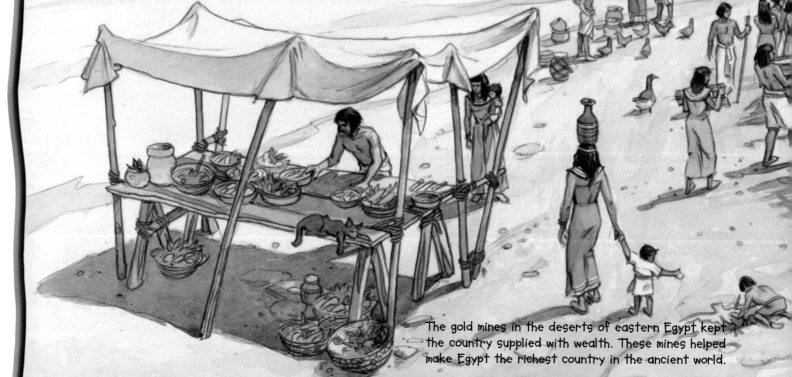

The gold mines in the deserts of eastern Egypt kept the country supplied with wealth. These mines helped make Egypt the richest country in the ancient world.

39 Egyptians traded with Syria, Lebanon, Palestine and Cyprus and with several African countries. Traders brought back silver from Syria, cedar wood, oils and horses from Lebanon, copper from Cyprus, a gem called lapis lazuli from Afghanistan, and ebony wood and ivory from central Africa.

I DON'T BELIEVE IT!
Fly swatters made from giraffe tails were a popular fashion item in ancient Egypt.

The Egyptians travelled to the land of Punt to bring back incense. We do not know exactly where the land of Punt is today, but we know that the Egyptians thought of it as a far away and exciting place.

40 When goods were sold they were weighed using a balance and special copper weights called deben. An item could be exchanged for its equivalent weight in copper. A bed, for example, had a value of 25 deben. Pieces of gold and silver were also weighed and used as payment.

The farmer's year

41 The farming year was divided into three seasons: the flood, the growing period and the harvest. Most people worked on the land, but farmers could not work between July and November because the land was covered by flood waters. Instead, they went off to help build the pyramids and royal palaces.

42 The river Nile used to flood its banks in July each year. The flood waters left a strip of rich black soil, about 10 km wide, along each bank. Apart from these fertile strips and a few scattered oases, pools of water in the desert, the rest of the land was mainly just sand.

44 Water was lifted from the Nile using a device called a shaduf. It was a long pole with a wooden bucket hanging from a rope at one end, and a weight at the other. The pole was supported by a wooden frame. One person working alone could operate a shaduf.

Tax collectors would often decide how rich a person was by counting how many cattle he owned.

43 Egyptian farmers had to water their crops because of the hot, dry climate with no rain. They dug special channels around their fields along which the waters of the Nile could flow. In this way farmers could water their crops all year round. This was called irrigation, and it is still done today.

Almost no rain fell on the dry, dusty farmland of ancient Egypt. No crops would grow properly without the water from the Nile.

45 Farmers used wooden ploughs pulled by oxen to prepare the soil for planting. They also had wooden hoes. The seeds were mainly planted by hand. At harvest time, wooden sickles edged with stone teeth were used to cut the crops.

46 Harvesting the grain was only the start of the process. In the threshing room people would beat the grain to separate it from the chaff, the shell, of the grain. It was then winnowed. Men would throw the grain and chaff up into the air and fan away the chaff. The heavier grain dropped straight to the floor. The grain was then gathered up and taken to the granary to be stored.

47 Wheat and barley (for bread and beer) were the two main crops grown by the ancient Egyptians. They also grew grapes (for wine) and flax (to make linen). A huge variety of fruits and vegetables grew in the fertile soil, including dates, figs, cucumbers, melons, onions, peas, leeks and lettuces.

I DON'T BELIEVE IT!

Instead of using scarecrows, Egyptian farmers hired young boys to scare away the birds – they had to have a loud voice and a good aim with a slingshot!

winnowers separate the grain from the chaff

Farmers had to hand over part of their harvest each year as a tax payment. It was usually given to the local temple in exchange for use of the temple's land.

48 Egyptian farmers kept cattle as well as goats, sheep, ducks and geese. Some farmers kept bees to produce honey, which was used for sweetening cakes and other foods.

Getting around

49 The main method of transport in ancient Egypt was by boat along the river Nile. The Nile is the world's longest river. It flows across the entire length of the desert lands of Egypt.

50 The earliest kinds of boat were made from papyrus reeds. They were propelled by a long pole and, later on, by oars. Gradually, wooden boats replaced the reed ones, and sails were added.

These early boats were made of bundles of reeds tied together.

Alexandria
Tanis
Avaris
Giza
Saqqara
Memphis
El-Amarna
Valley of the Kings
Thebes
Karnak
Luxor
Aswan
LOWER NUBIA
Abu Simbel
UPPER NUBIA
Kerma
KUSH
Red Sea
Blue Nile
White Nile

▲ The total length of the river Nile is around 6,670 kilometres. To the south of Egypt, the Nile has two main branches – the White Nile and the Blue Nile.

51 A magnificent carved boat was built to carry the body of King Khufu at his funeral. Over 43 metres long, it was built from planks of cedar wood. The boat was buried in a special pit next to the Great Pyramid.

▼ The cabin on board Khufu's funerary boat was decorated with carved flowers. Other traditional designs were carved into the boat. The joints were held together with strips of leather.

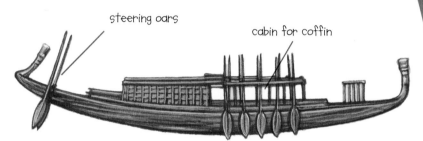

steering oars

cabin for coffin

52 Wooden barges carried blocks of limestone across the river Nile for the pyramids and temples. The stone came from quarries on the opposite bank to the site of the pyramids. The granite used to build the insides of the pyramids came from much farther away – from quarries at Aswan 800 kilometres upstream.

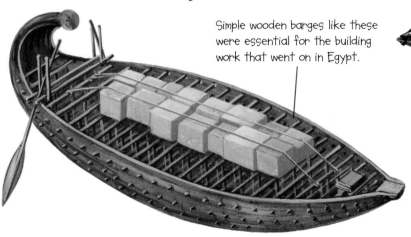

Simple wooden barges like these were essential for the building work that went on in Egypt.

QUIZ 2

How well do you know your gods and goddesses? Can you name these:

1. This god has a jackal's head and hangs around dead bodies.

2. This god's magic eye will protect you from evil.

3. Cats are really fond of this goddess.

4. This god is a bit of a snappy character!

1. Anubis 2. Horus 3. Bastet 4. Sobek

53 Wooden–built trading ships were propelled by a combination of sail and oar power. Wide-bodied cargo boats were used to ferry cattle across the Nile. The animals stood on deck during the crossing.

Who's who in Ancient Egypt

54 The people of ancient Egypt were organized into three classes: upper, middle and lower. The royal family, government officials, senior priests and priestesses, scribes and doctors made up the upper class. Traders, merchants and craftworkers were middle class. The biggest group of people by far – the unskilled workers – made up the lower class.

◀ The arrangement of Egyptian society can be shown as a pyramid shape. The pharaoh sits at the top of the pyramid, with the huge mass of unskilled labourers at the bottom.

viziers and priests

scribes and noblemen

craftworkers and dancers

carrying grain from the fields

peasant workers winnowing grain

55 The man was the head of any Egyptian household. On his father's death, the eldest son inherited the family's land and riches. Egyptian women had rights and privileges too. They could own property and carry out businesses deals, and women from wealthy families could become doctors or priestesses.

Memphis
Thebes

Egypt, Old Kingdom

Memphis
Thebes

Egypt, Middle Kingdom

Memphis
Thebes

Egypt, New Kingdom

▲ These maps show the extent of the Egyptian empire in the three kingdoms.

56 Most ancient Egyptians lived along the banks of the river Nile or in the river valley. As Egypt became more powerful they spread out, up along the river Nile and around the Mediterranean Sea. Others lived by oases, pools of water in the desert.

57 Rich families had several servants, who worked as maids, cooks and gardeners. In large houses the servants had their own quarters separate from those of the family.

58 Dogs and cats were the main family pets. Egyptians also kept pet monkeys and sometimes flocks of tame doves. Some people trained their pet baboons to climb fig trees and pick the ripe fruits.

▲ Family life played an important role in ancient Egypt. Couples could adopt children if they were unable to have their own.

59 Young children played with wooden and clay toys. Popular toys were carved animals – often with moving parts – spinning tops, toy horses, dolls and clay balls. Children also played games which are still played today, such as leapfrog and tug-o'-war.

I DON'T BELIEVE IT!

Wealthy Egyptians wanted servants in the afterlife too. They were buried with models of servants, called shabtis, that were meant to come to life and look after their dead owner!

Home sweet home

60 Egyptian houses were made from mud bricks dried in the sun. Mud was taken from the river Nile, and straw and pebbles were added to make it stronger. The trunks of palm trees supported the flat roofs. The inside walls of houses were covered with plaster, and often painted. Wealthy Egyptians lived in large houses with several storeys. A poorer family, though, might live in a crowded single room.

◀ A mixture of mud, straw and stones was poured into wooden frames or shaped into bricks and left to harden in the sun.

61 In most Egyptian homes there was a small shrine. Here, members of the family worshipped their household god.

The dwarf god, Bes, was the ancient Egyptian god of children and the home.

62 Egyptians furnished their homes with wooden stools, chairs, tables, storage chests and carved beds. A low three- or four-legged footstool was one of the most popular items of furniture. Mats of woven reeds covered the floors.

63 Rich families lived in spacious villas in the countryside. A typical villa had a pond filled with fish, a walled garden and an orchard of fruit trees.

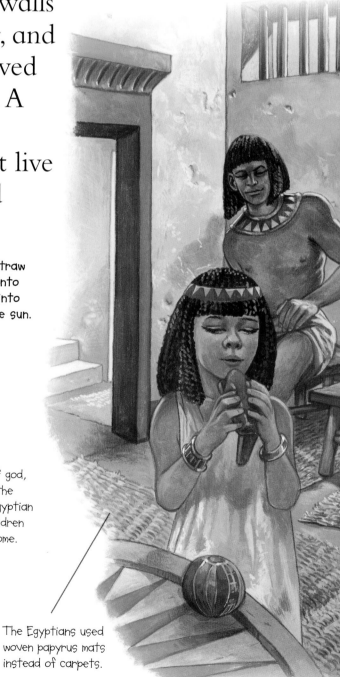

The Egyptians used woven papyrus mats instead of carpets.

64 They cooked their food in a clay oven or over an open fire. Most kitchens were equipped with a cylinder-shaped oven made from bricks of baked clay. They burned either charcoal or wood as fuel. They cooked food in two-handled pottery saucepans.

Senet was a popular board game in ancient Egypt. Experts today think it was probably a bit like ludo.

QUIZ 3

1. Why did the Egyptians bury a boat next to their pharaoh?
2. Which part of the body was left inside a mummy?
3. Who was Howard Carter?
4. Why did farmworkers have nothing to do between July and November each year?

1. So he can use it in the next life 2. The heart 3. The man who discovered the tomb of Tutankhamun 4. The river Nile had flooded the farmland

65 Pottery lamps provided the lighting in Egyptian homes. They filled the container with oil and burned a wick made of cotton or flax. Houses had very small windows, and sometimes none at all, so there was often very little natural light. Small windows kept out the strong sunlight, helping to keep houses cool.

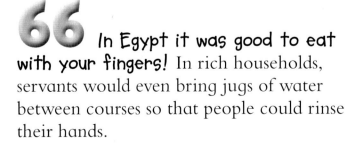

66 In Egypt it was good to eat with your fingers! In rich households, servants would even bring jugs of water between courses so that people could rinse their hands.

Dressing up

67 **Egyptians wore lucky charms called amulets.** The charms were meant to protect the wearer from evil spirits and to bring good luck. One of the most popular ones was the wadjat eye of the god Horus. Children wore amulets shaped like fish to protect them from drowning in the river Nile.

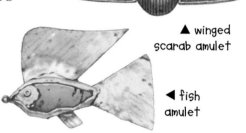

◄ The eye of Horus was thought to protect everything behind it. The god Horus had his eye torn out while defending the throne of Egypt. Later, the eye was magically repaired.

▲ winged scarab amulet

◄ fish amulet

68 **In Egypt, men and women both wore eye make-up.** A special black eye make-up, called kohl, was made from ground-up raw metals mixed with oil. The Egyptians believed it had magical healing powers and could restore bad eyesight and fight eye infections. Egyptians also used face rouge for the cheeks and lips, face powder, paint for fingernails and hair dyes.

wig and box

make-up box

69 Most clothes were made from light-coloured linen.
Women wore long dresses, oftern with pleated cloaks. Noblewomen's dresses were made of the best cloth with beads sewn onto it. Men wore either robes or kilt-like skirts, a piece of linen wrapped around the waist and tied in a decorative knot.

▶ This fine long dress is worn with a see-through cloak. Clothes like these made sure that the people of Egypt kept cool in the hot weather.

MAKE A MAGIC EYE CHARM

You will need

self-hardening modelling clay
a length of leather strip or thick cord
a pencil   poster paints
a paintbrush   varnish

Knead the clay until soft and then shape into a wadjat eye. Add extra clay for the pupil of the eye and at the top of the charm. Use the pencil to make the top piece into a loop.

Leave the clay to harden. Paint in bright colours and leave to dry. Varnish. Thread the leather strip or cord through the loop and wear your charm for extra luck.

70 Wealthy people wore wigs made from human hair or sheep's wool which they kept in special boxes on stands at home. Girls wore their hair in pigtails, while boys mostly had shaved heads, sometimes with a plaited lock on one side.

wigs

comb

hair pins

comb

▲ Wigs were often long and elaborate and needed a lot of attention. Egyptians cared for their wigs with combs made of wood and ivory. They sometimes used curling tongs as well.

71 Sandals were made from papyrus and other reeds.
Rich people, courtiers and kings and queens wore padded leather ones. Footwear was a luxury item, and most ordinary people walked around barefoot. Colourful pictures of sandals were even painted onto the feet of mummies!

▼ leather sandals

▼ reed sandals

Baking and brewing

72 **Bread was the most important food in the diet of ancient Egypt.** Harvested grain was stored in huge granaries until needed. The Egyptians' favourite drink was beer. It was very thick and had to be strained before drinking. Models of brewers were even left in tombs to make sure the dead person had a plentiful supply of beer in the next world!

▼ An Egyptian banquet was a real occasion! Rich people could afford the best food and drink, but they would also have servants, as well as musicians and dancers.

73 A rough kind of bread was baked from either wheat or barley. The bread often contained gritty pieces that wore down the teeth of the Egyptians. Historians have discovered this by studying the teeth of mummies.

DESIGN A BANQUET MENU

A huge choice of foods was served at banquets for wealthy Egyptians. Meats such as duck, goose, gazelle and heron, fresh fruits and vegetables, sweet pastries and cakes, with lots of beer and grape or date wine to drink.

Choose the foods for a banquet and design a decorative menu for your guests.

Hard day's work

74 Scribes were very important people in ancient Egypt. These highly skilled men kept records of everything that happened from day to day. They recorded all the materials used for building work, the numbers of cattle, and the crops that had been gathered for the royal family, the government and the temples.

◀ Only the sons of scribes could undergo the strict scribe training, which began as early as the age of nine.

75 The libraries of ancient Egypt held thousands of papyrus scrolls. They covered subjects such as astronomy, medicine, geography and law. Most ordinary Egyptians could not read or write, so the libraries were used only by educated people such as scribes and doctors.

76 Imagine if there were 700 letters in the alphabet! That was how many hieroglyphs Egyptian schoolchildren had to learn! Hieroglyphs were symbols that the Egyptians used for writing. Some symbols stood for words and some for sounds. Children went to schools for scribes where they first learned how to read and write hieroglyphs.

▼ Craftworkers produced statues and furniture for the pharoah. Workers such as these often had their own areas within a town. The village of Deir el-Medina was built specially for those who worked on tombs in the Valley of the Kings.

77 Most people worked as craftworkers or farm labourers. Craftworkers included carpenters, potters, weavers, jewellers, shoemakers, glassblowers and perfume makers. Many sold their goods from small shops in the towns. They were kept busy making items for the pharaoh and wealthy people.

78 A typical lunch for a worker consisted of bread and onions. They may also have had a cucumber, washed down with a drink of beer.

QUIZ 4

Can you name the following items from life in ancient Egypt?

1.
2.
3.
4.

1.The dwarf god Bes 2. A canopic jar 3. A hair comb 4. An amulet

79 The base of the Great Pyramid takes up almost as much space as five football pitches! Huge quantities of stone were needed to build these monuments. The Egyptians quarried limestone, sandstone and granite for their buildings. In the surrounding desert they mined gold for decorations.

80 Slaves were often prisoners who had been captured from Egypt's enemies. They also came from the neighbouring countries of Kush and Nubia. Life as a slave was not all bad. A slave could own land and buy goods – he could even buy his freedom!

Clever Egyptians

81 The insides of many Egyptian tombs were decorated with brightly coloured wall paintings. They often depicted scenes from the dead person's life, showing him or her as a healthy young person. The Egyptians believed that these scenes would come to life in the next world.

sunken relief

▶ The Egyptians produced raised reliefs by cutting away the background, and sunken relief by cutting stone from inside the outline.

raised relief

82 Egyptian sculptors carved enormous stone statues of their pharaohs and gods. These were often placed outside a tomb or temple to guard the entrance. Scenes, called reliefs, were carved into the walls of temples and tombs. These often showed the person as they were when they were young, enjoying scenes from daily life. This was so that when the god Osiris brought the dead person and the tomb paintings back to life, the tomb owners would have a good time in the afterlife!

83 The ancient Egyptians had three different calendars: an everyday farming one, an astronomical and a lunar (Moon) calendar. The 365-day farming calendar was made up of three seasons of four months. The astronomical calendar was based on observations of the star Sirius, which reappeared each year at the start of the flood season. Priests kept a calendar based on the movements of the Moon which told them when to perform ceremonies for to the moon god Khonsu.

▲ The days on this calendar are written in black and red. Black days are ordinary, but the red days are unlucky.

◄ Several artists worked on the tomb paintings. A junior artist drew the outlines of the scene, which were then checked and corrected by a more senior artist. Next, painters filled in the outlines in colour.

84 Astronomers recorded their observations of the night skies.

The Egyptian calendar was based on the movement of Sirius, the brightest star in the sky. The Egyptians used their knowledge of astronomy to build temples which lined up with certain stars or with the movement of the Sun.

I DON'T BELIEVE IT!

Bulbs of garlic were used to ward off snakes and to get rid of tapeworms from people's bodies.

85 Egyptian doctors knew how to set broken bones and treat illnesses such as fevers.

They used medicines made from plants such as garlic and juniper to treat sick people. The Egyptians had a good knowledge of the basic workings of the human body.

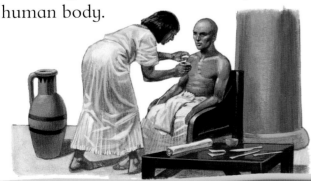

86 The Egyptians used a device called a nilometer to measure the depth of the river Nile.

They inserted measuring posts into the riverbed at intervals along the bank so they could check the water levels at the start of each flood season.

From pictures to words

87 **The Egyptians had no paper – they wrote on papyrus.** It was made from the tall papyrus reeds that grew on the banks of the Nile. At first papyrus was sold as long strips, or scrolls, tied with string. Later the Egyptians put the papyrus sheets into books. Papyrus is very long lasting; sheets of papyrus have survived 3,000 years to the present day.

88 **Ink was made by mixing water with soot, charcoal or coloured minerals.** Scribes wrote in ink on papyrus scrolls, using reed brushes with specially shaped ends.

1. Papyrus was expensive because it took a long time to make. First people had to cut down the papyrus stems, and cut them up into lots of thin strips.

2. Then someone laid these strips in rows on a frame to form layers.

3. The papyrus strips were then pressed under weights. This squeezed out the water and squashed the layers together.

4. Finally, when the papyrus was dry, a man with a stone rubbed the surface smooth for writing.

89

The Rosetta Stone was found in 1799 by a French soldier in Egypt. It is a large slab of stone onto which three different kinds of writing have been carved: hieroglyphics, a simpler form of hieroglyphics called demotic and Greek. All three sets of writing give an account of the coronation of King Ptolemy V. By translating the Greek, scholars could understand the Egyptian writing for the first time.

90

The ancient Egyptians used a system of picture writing called hieroglyphics. Each hieroglyph represented an object or a sound. For example, the picture of a lion represented the sound 'l'; a basket represented the word 'lord'. Altogether there were about 700 different hieroglyphs. Scribes wrote them on papyrus scrolls or carved them into stone.

91

In the 5th century BC a Greek historian called Herodotus wrote about life in ancient Egypt. As he travelled across the country he oberved and wrote about people's daily lives, and their religion and customs such as embalming and mummification – he even wrote about cats!

WRITE YOUR NAME IN HIEROGLYPHICS

Below you will see the hieroglyphic alphabet. I have written my name in hieroglyphs. Can you write yours?

J A N E

A	B	C	D	E	F	G	H

I	J	K	L	M	N	O	P

Q	R	S	T	U	V	W	X	Y	Z

92

The hieroglyphs of a ruler's name were written inside an oval-shaped frame called a cartouche. The pharaoh's cartouche was carved on pillars and temple walls, painted on tomb walls and mummy cases and written on official documents.

Fun and games

93 Hippo hunting was a dangerous but popular sport in ancient Egypt. Hunters in reed boats, armed only with spears and ropes, killed hippos in the waters of the Nile. In the desert, hunters chased lions, antelope, wild bulls, gazelles and hares. Marsh birds were killed with throwing sticks that were like boomerangs.

▲ Hunting was reserved mostly for royalty and courtiers. Amenhotep III was said to have killed more than 100 lions in 10 years.

MAKE A SNAKE GAME
You will need

a sheet of thick cardboard
a large dinner plate a paintbrush
scissors coloured pens
white paint counters
a pencil two dice

Place the plate on the card
and draw round the
outside. Cut out the
circle. Paint one side
with paint. Leave
to dry.

Draw a snake's head in
the centre of the board. Draw
small circles (about 2 cm across)
spreading out from the centre until you
reach the edge of the board. Colour the
circles to make an attractive pattern.

Place a counter for each player on the
outside square. The winner is the first
player to reach the snake's head.

94 The Egyptians played
various board games, a few of which
we still play today. The game of senet
was supposed to represent the struggle
between good and evil on the journey
into the next world. Players moved sets of
counters across the board according to
how their throwing sticks (like modern
dice) landed. Another popular board
game was called hounds and jackals.

Heroes and heroines

95 **Ramses II built more temples than any other Egyptian ruler.** Two of his greatest achievements are the huge rock-cut temple at Abu Simbel and the Great Hall at Karnak. He also finished building the mortuary temple of Seti I at Luxor. After his death a further nine pharaohs were given the name Ramses.

Lapis lazuli is a bright-blue semi-precious gem that the Egyptians used to decorate the coffins of rich people.

▼ The Great Hall at Karnak

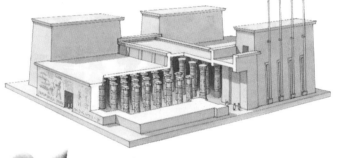

96 **Queen Hatshepsut was often depicted wearing men's clothing and a false beard.** She was the wife of Thutmose II. On his death Hatshepsut took the title of pharaoh and adopted the royal symbols of the double crown, the crook, the flail (whip) – and also the ceremonial beard!

▶ During her 20-year reign Hatshepsut sent an expedition of five ships to Punt on the coast of the Red Sea. The ships brought back incense, copper and ivory.

Mark Antony   Cleopatra

97 **Queen Cleopatra VII was one of the last rulers of ancient Egypt.** She fell in love with the Roman emperor Julius Caesar, and later married the Roman general Mark Antony. Cleopatra killed herself in 30 BC when the Romans conquered Egypt.

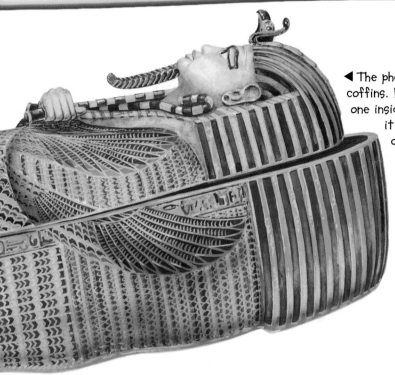

◄ The pharaoh Tutankhamun was buried in three separate coffins. Each coffin was specially made to go around the one inside. This is the middle coffin. Like all the coffins, it is made of gold, but this one is also inlaid with a gem called lapis lazuli.

Narmer palette

100 King Menes was the first ruler of a united Egypt.
He joined together the kingdoms of Upper and Lower Egypt, under one government, in around 3100 BC. Menes was also called Narmer. Archaeologists have found a slate tablet, called the Narmer Palette, that shows him beating his enemies in battle.

98 Tutankhamun is probably the most famous pharaoh of all.
His tomb, with its fabulous treasure of over 5,000 objects, was discovered complete in 1922. Tutankhamun was only nine years old when he became ruler, and he died at the young age of about 17. He was buried in the Valley of the Kings.

99 Thutmose III was a clever general who added new lands to ancient Egypt.
Under his leadership, Egypt's armies seized territory in Syria to the north and Palestine to the east. During his reign Thutmose ordered a giant obelisk made of granite to be placed at Heliopolis — it now stands on the bank of the river Thames in London.

QUIZ 5

1. Name two popular drinks in ancient Egypt.

2. What is a cartouche?

3. What is the Rosetta Stone?

4. What is senet?

5. Explain why Queen Hatshepsut was unusual.

1. Beer and wine 2. An oval plaque on which the pharaoh's name was written. 3. The stone that enabled historians to read hieroglyphs. 4. An ancient Egyptian game. 5. She ruled as a pharaoh, wearing the ceremonial beard.

The centre of an empire

101 Rome was a city in central Italy that ruled one the world's greatest empires. An empire is made up of many different countries governed by a single ruler. Rome began around 1000BC as a village of wooden huts, but soon grew rich and powerful. It was busy, crowded, noisy and exciting, with many beautiful buildings. By 200BC the Romans ruled most of Italy, and started to invade neighbouring lands. They conquered a vast empire that stretched between what we now call Scotland and Turkey.

51

Capital city

102 **Over a million people lived in the city of Rome.** By around AD300, Rome was the largest city in the world. There were citizens who could vote and serve in the army, and there were non-citizens who did not have these rights. The government was run by nobles and knights who were usually very rich. Plebeians, or ordinary people, were usually fairly poor but were citizens of Rome. Slaves were not citizens. They were not free and they had no rights.

103 The Forum was the government are in the centre of Rome. People went there to meet their friends and business colleagues, discuss politics, and to listen to famous orators who made speeches in the open air. The Forum was mainly a market-place, surrounded by government buildings such as offices and law-courts.

104 Rome was a well-protected city. It was surrounded by 50 kilometres of strong stone walls, to keep out attackers. All visitors had to enter the city through one of its 37 gates which were guarded by soldiers and watchmen.

105 The Romans were great water engineers. They designed aqueducts, channels to carry water from streams in far-away hills and mountains to the city. The richest Roman homes were supplied with constant running water carried in lead pipes. Ordinary people had to drink from public fountains.

106 Rome relied on its drains. Rome was so crowded that good drains were essential. Otherwise, the citizens could have caught diseases from sewage and died. The largest sewer, the 'cloaca maxima', was so high and so wide that a horse and cart could drive through it.

I DON'T BELIEVE IT!

Roman engineers also designed public lavatories. These lavatories were convenient, but not private. Users sat on rows of seats, side by side!

City life

107 **The Romans built the world's first high-rise apartments.** Most of the people who lived in Ostia, a busy port close to Rome, had jobs connected with trade, such as shipbuilders and money-changers. They lived in blocks of flats known as 'insulae'. A typical block was three or four storeys high, with up to a hundred small, dirty, crowded rooms.

108 **Rich Romans had more than one home.** Rome was stuffy, dirty and smelly, especially in summer time. Wealthy Roman families liked to get away from the city to cleaner, more peaceful surroundings. They purchased a house (a 'villa urbana') just outside the city, or a big house surrounded by farmland (a 'villa rustica') in the countryside far away from Rome.

109 **Many Roman homes had a pool, but it was not used for swimming!** Pools were built for decoration, in the central courtyards of large Roman homes. They were surrounded by plants and statues. Some pools had a fountain; others had mosaics – pictures made of tiny coloured stones or squares of glass – covering the floor.

MAKE A PAPER MOSAIC

You will need:

large sheet of paper   scissors
pencil   glue
scraps of coloured and textured paper

Draw the outlines of your design on a large sheet of paper. Plan which colours to use for different parts of the mosaic.

Cut the paper scraps into small squares, all roughly the same size. The simplest way to do this is to cut strips, then snip the strips into squares.

Stick the paper squares onto the large sheet of paper following the outlines of your design.

110 Fortunate families had hot feet.
Homes belonging to wealthy families had underfloor central heating. Blasts of hot air, warmed by a wood-burning furnace, circulated in channels built beneath the floor. The furnace was kept burning by slaves who chopped wood and stoked the fire.

space in walls for hot air to circulate

fire for heating

space under the floor for hot air

111 Rome had its own fire brigade.
The 7,000 firemen were all specially trained freed slaves. Ordinary families could not afford central heating, so they warmed their rooms with fires in big clay pots which often set the house alight.

Going shopping

112 Rome housed the world's first shopping mall. It was called Trajan's Market, and was built on five different levels on the slopes of the Quirinal Hill in the centre of Rome. It contained over 150 different shops together with a large main hall.

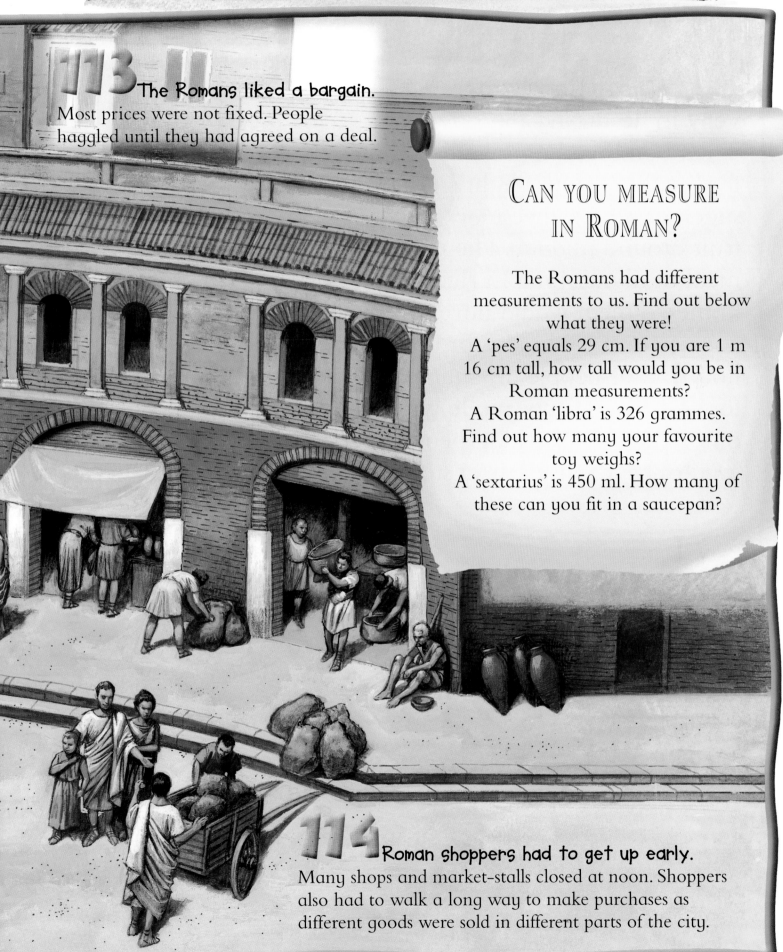

113 The Romans liked a bargain.

Most prices were not fixed. People haggled until they had agreed on a deal.

CAN YOU MEASURE IN ROMAN?

The Romans had different measurements to us. Find out below what they were!
A 'pes' equals 29 cm. If you are 1 m 16 cm tall, how tall would you be in Roman measurements?
A Roman 'libra' is 326 grammes. Find out how many your favourite toy weighs?
A 'sextarius' is 450 ml. How many of these can you fit in a saucepan?

114 Roman shoppers had to get up early.

Many shops and market-stalls closed at noon. Shoppers also had to walk a long way to make purchases as different goods were sold in different parts of the city.

Eating and drinking

115 Most Romans ate very little during the day. They had bread and water for breakfast and a light snack of bread, cheese or fruit around midday. They ate their main meal at about 4pm. In rich people's homes, a meal would have three separate courses, and could last for up to three hours! Poor people ate much simpler foods, such as soups made with lentils and onions, barley porridge, peas, cabbage and tough, cheap cuts of meat stewed in vinegar.

116 Only rich Roman people had their own kitchen. They could afford to employ a chef with slaves to help him in the kitchen. Ordinary people went to 'popinae' (cheap eating houses) for their main meal, or bought ready-cooked snacks from roadside fast food stalls.

117 At parties, the Romans ate lying down. Men and women lay on long couches arranged round a table. They also often wore crowns of flowers, and took off their sandals before entering the dining room. Nine was the ideal number of guests for a dinner party, but many people had more.

REAL ROMAN FOOD!

PATINA DE PIRIS (Pear Soufflé)
Ingredients:

1kg pears (peeled and cored)	a little bit of oil
	pinch of salt
	$\frac{1}{2}$ tsp cumin
6 eggs (beaten)	ground pepper
4 tblsp honey	to taste

Make sure that you ask an adult to help you with this recipe.
Mash the pears together with the pepper, cumin, honey, and a bit of oil. Add the beaten eggs and put into a casserole. Cook for approximately 30 minutes in a moderate oven. Serve with a little bit of pepper sprinkled on top.

▼ Dishes served at a Roman banquet might include shellfish, roast meat, eggs, vegetables, fresh fruits, pastries and honeyed wine. The Romans enjoyed strong-flavoured, spicy food, and also sweet–sour flavours.

School days

118 **Roman boys learned how to speak well.** Roman schools taught three main subjects, reading, maths – and public speaking! Boys needed all three skills for their future careers. There were no newspapers or television, so politicians, army leaders and government officials all had to make speeches in public, explaining their plans and policies to Roman crowds. Boys went to school from around seven years old and left aged 16.

▼ Roman schoolboys practise reading with their slave schoolmaster.

119 **Roman girls did not go to school.** They mostly stayed at home, where their mothers, or women slaves, taught them how to cook, clean, weave cloth and look after children. Girls from rich families, or families who ran a business, also learned to read, write and keep accounts.

▼ A girl is taught to play the lyre.

120 **Many of the best teachers were slaves.** Schoolmasters and private tutors often came from Greece. They were purchased by wealthy people who wanted to give their sons a good education. The Greeks had a long tradition of learning, which the Romans admired.

121 The Romans wrote a lot – but not on paper.

They used thin slices of wood for letters and day-to-day business. For notes Romans used flat wooden boards covered with wax, as the wax could be smoothed over and used again. For important documents that they wanted to keep, the Romans used cleaned and polished calfskin, or papyrus.

ink pot

pens

wax tablet

stylus, to use with a wax tablet

122 Romans made ink from soot.

To make black ink, the Romans mixed soot from wood fires with vinegar and a sticky gum that oozed from the bark of trees. This sounds like a strange mixture, but some Roman writing has survived for almost 2,000 years.

123 Rome had many libraries.

Some were public, and open to everyone, others belonged to rich families and were kept shut away in their houses. It was fashionable to sponsor writers and collect their works.

124 Many Romans read standing up – it was easier that way.

It took time and patience to learn how to read from a papyrus scroll. Most were at least 10 metres long. Readers held the scroll in their right hand, and a stick in their left hand. They unrolled a small section of the scroll at a time.

LEARN SOME ROMAN WORDS!

The Romans spoke a language called Latin. It forms the basis of many languages today, and below you can learn some Latin for yourself!

liber = book   epistola = letter
bibliotheca = library
vellum = calfskin
stylus = writing stick
(used with wax tablets)
librarii = slaves who work in a library
grammaticus = schoolmaster
paedagogus = private tutor

Father knows best!

125 A Roman father had the power of life and death over his family. According to Roman law, each family had to be headed by a man. He was known as the 'paterfamilias' (father of a family), and was usually the oldest surviving male. The buildings of the house and its contents belonged to him, and he had the right to punish any family members who misbehaved. Even his mother and other older female relatives were expected to obey him.

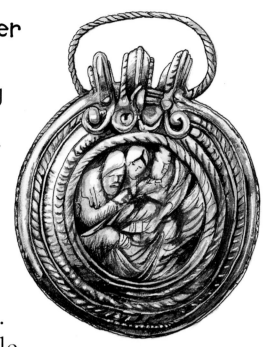

▲ The Romans gave a good luck charm, called a bulla, to their babies.

126 Roman families included more than blood relations. To the Romans, a 'family' meant all the people living and working together in the same household. So families included many different slaves and servants, as well as a husband and wife and their children.

▲ This carving shows a Roman wedding, the bride and groom are in the centre, with a priestess behind them.

I DON'T BELIEVE IT!

The Romans invented Valentine's Day, but called it Lupercalia. Boys picked a girl's name from a hat, and she was meant to be their girlfriend for the year!

127 **Sons were valued more than daughters.** Boys would grow up to carry on the family name. They might also bring fame and honour to a family by achievements in politics and war. They might marry a rich wife, which helped to make the whole family richer, or win friends among powerful people.

128 **Childhood was short for a Roman girl.** Roman law allowed girls to get married at 12 years old, and many had become mothers by the time they were 15. Roman girls could not choose whom to marry, especially if they came from rich or powerful families. Instead, marriages were arranged by families, to gain political power or encourage business deals. Love was not important.

129 **Roman families liked to keep pets.** Roman statues and paintings show many children playing with their pets. Dogs, cats and doves were all popular. Some families also kept ornamental fish and tame deer.

Roman style

130 **Most Roman clothes were made without sewing.** Roman men and women wore loose-fitting robes, made of long strips of cloth. They were draped round the body, and held in place by pins, brooches or belts. Most women wore several layers. These were a thin shift, a 'tunica', a long, sleeveless dress called a 'stola', and a thick cloak called a 'palla'. Men wore a knee-length tunic, a 'colobium', with a semi-circular cloak, a 'toga', over the top.

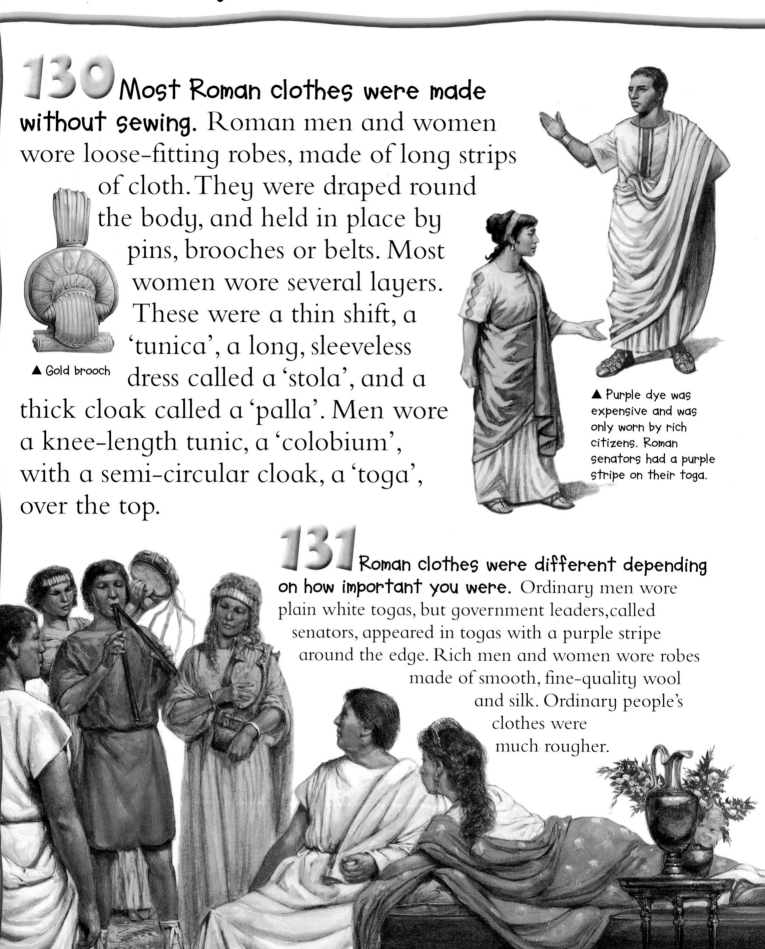

▲ Gold brooch

▲ Purple dye was expensive and was only worn by rich citizens. Roman senators had a purple stripe on their toga.

131 **Roman clothes were different depending on how important you were.** Ordinary men wore plain white togas, but government leaders, called senators, appeared in togas with a purple stripe around the edge. Rich men and women wore robes made of smooth, fine-quality wool and silk. Ordinary people's clothes were much rougher.

◄ This Celtic warrior from northern Europe has used dye from a plant called woad as war–paint on his body.

132 **Clothes told the world who you were.** People from many different cultures and races lived in lands ruled by the Romans. They wore many different styles of clothes. For example, men from Egypt wore wigs and short linen kilts. Celtic women from northern Europe wore long woollen shawls, woven in brightly coloured checks. Celtic men wore trousers.

▼ These Roman sandals have metal studs in the soles to make sure that they don't wear down too quickly!

DRESS LIKE A ROMAN!

You can wear your very own toga! Ask an adult for a blanket or a sheet, then follow the instructions below!

First ask an adult to find you a blanket or sheet. White is best, like the Romans.

Drape your sheet over your left shoulder. Now pass the rest behind your back.

Pull the sheet across your front, so that you're wrapped up in it. You're almost a Roman now!

Finally, drape the last end over your right hand and there you have it, a Roman toga!

133 **Roman boots were made for walking!** Roman soldiers and travellers wore lace-up boots with thick leather soles studded with iron nails. Other Roman footwear included 'socci', loose-fitting slippers to wear indoors. Farmers wore shoes made of a single piece of ox-hide wrapped round the foot, called 'carbatinae'. There were also 'crepidae', comfortable lace-up sandals with open toes.

Looking good

134 **Just like today, hairstyles changed according to fashion.** All free-born Roman women grew their hair long as short hair was a sign of slavery. In early Roman times the fashion was for plain and simple styles. Later on, most women wore their hair smoothed down and tied back tightly. Roman men usually wore short hair, and were mostly clean-shaven, except when they were old.

◄ Rich women spent a lot of time on their hair. Pins of ivory and bone were used to keep some elaborate styles in place.

135 **The Romans painted their faces.** The Romans admired pale, smooth skin. Women, and some men, used stick-on patches of cloth called 'splenia' to cover spots, and wore lots of make-up. They used crushed chalk or white lead as face-powder, red ochre (crumbly earth) for blusher, plant juice for lipstick and wood-ash or powdered antimony (a silvery metal) as eye-liner.

136 Blonde hair was highly prized.

Most Romans were born with wiry dark brown hair. Some fashionable people admired delicate blonde hair, because it was unusual. Roman women used vinegar and lye (an early form of soap, made from urine and wood-ash) to bleach their own hair.

137 Going to the barbers could be very painful.

In Roman times, sharp scissors and razors had not been invented. Barbers used shears to trim men's hair and beards. When a smooth, close-shaven look was in fashion barbers had to pull men's beards out by the roots, one hair at a time!

QUIZ

If you had to dress up as a Roman, what clothes would you wear? Use the information on these pages to help you draw a picture of the clothes you would need and how you might arrange your hair. Will you be a rich governor, a Celtic warrior or a soldier?

138 Romans liked to smell sweet.

They used olive oil (made from the crushed fruit of the olive tree) to cleanse and soften their skins, and perfumes to scent their bodies. Ingredients for perfume came from many different lands – flowers came from southern Europe, spices came from India and Africa and sweet-smelling bark and resin came from Arabia.

olive oil

flowers to make perfume

bark used for perfume

star anise to make perfume

olives

ash to darken eyelids

saffron for eyeshadow

perfume bottle made of onyx, a kind of black stone

139 Roman combs were made from bone, ivory or wood.

Like combs today, they were designed to smooth and untangle hair, and were sometimes worn as hair ornaments. But they had another, less pleasant, purpose – they were used for combing out all the little nits and lice!

Bath time

140 The Romans went to the public baths in order to relax. These huge buildings were more than a place to get clean. They were also fitness centres and places to meet friends. Visitors could take part in sports, such as wrestling, do exercises, have a massage or a haircut. They could buy scented oils and perfumes, read a book, eat a snack or admire works of art in the baths own sculpture gallery!

▼ There were public baths in most districts of Rome. They were built by Roman emperors or rich families as a gift to the citizens. The finest were the baths of Caracalla (opened around AD215), which had room for 1,600 bathers at a time.

The 'frigidarium' had the coldest pool.

141 **Families could not bathe together.** Roman men and women did not take baths together, not even husbands and wives. Women usually went to the baths in the mornings, while most men were at work. Men went to the baths in the afternoons.

The 'tepidarium' had a cool, or tepid, pool.

The hot room was called the 'caldarium'.

Fires heat the water for the hot rooms.

142 **Bathing wasn't simple.** There were five separate stages to taking a bath Roman-style. After changing, bathers went into a very hot room, which was full of steam where they sat for a while. Then they went into a hot, dry room, where a slave removed all the sweat and dirt from their skin, using a metal scraper and olive oil. To cool off, they went for a swim in a tepid pool. Finally, they jumped into a bracing cold pool.

Having fun

143 The Romans liked music and dancing.
Groups of buskers played in the streets, or
could be hired to perform at private parties.
Among ordinary families, favourite
instruments included pipes, flutes, cymbals,
castanets and horns. Rich, well-educated
people, though, thought the noise they
made was vulgar. They
preferred the quieter, gentler
sound of the lyre, which
was played to accompany
poets and singers.

▲ Roman buskers play music
in the street.

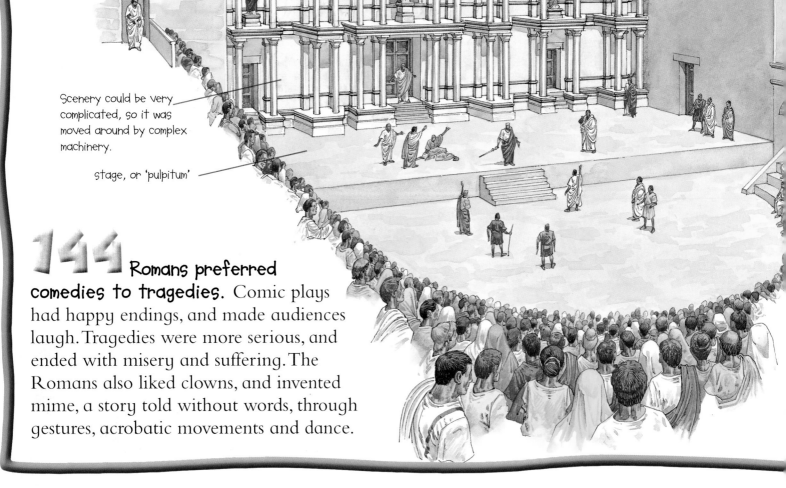

Scenery could be very
complicated, so it was
moved around by complex
machinery.

stage, or 'pulpitum'

144 Romans preferred
comedies to tragedies. Comic plays
had happy endings, and made audiences
laugh. Tragedies were more serious, and
ended with misery and suffering. The
Romans also liked clowns, and invented
mime, a story told without words, through
gestures, acrobatic movements and dance.

145 Plays were originally part of religious festivals. Many famous dramas showed scenes from ancient myths and legends, and were designed to make people think about morals and politics. Later, plays were written on all sorts of topics – including politics and current affairs. Some were paid for by rich politicians, to spread their political message. They handed out free tickets to Roman citizens, hoping to win votes.

147 Roman actors all wore masks. Masks helped the audience in big theatres see what each character was feeling. They were carved and painted in bright colours, with larger than life features and exaggerated expressions. Some masks were happy, some were frightened, some were sad.

148 Other favourite pastimes included games of skill and chance. Roman adults and children enjoyed dice and knucklebones, which needed nimble fingers, and draughts which relied on luck and quick thinking. They played these for fun, but adults also made bets on who would win.

◄ All the parts in Roman plays were performed by men. For women's roles, men wore masks and dressed in female costume. Women could not be actors, except in mime.

146 Theatres were huge well-built structures. One of the best preserved Roman theatres is at Orange, in southern France. It has seats for almost 10,000 people. It is so cleverly designed, that the audience can hear the actors even from the back row.

I DON'T BELIEVE IT!

Roman actors were almost all men. Some were as popular as TV stars today. Women couldn't sit near the stage, in case they tried to arrange a date with one of the stars!

Let the games begin!

149 Romans admired gladiators for their strength, bravery and skill. However, gladiators' lives were short and their deaths were horrible. They were sent to the arena to fight – and suffer – until they died.

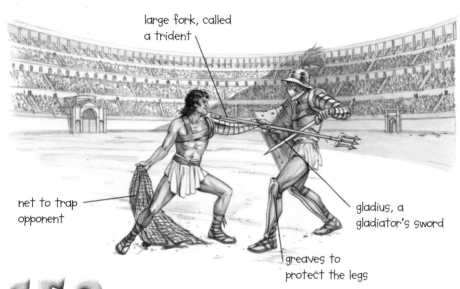

large fork, called a trident

net to trap opponent

gladius, a gladiator's sword

greaves to protect the legs

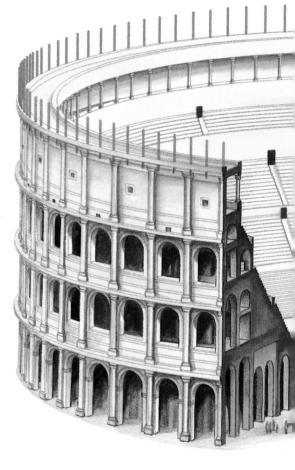

150 Most gladiators did not choose to fight. They were either prisoners-of-war or criminals who were sold to fight-trainers who organised gladiator shows. Some were specially trained, so that they would survive for longer and provide better entertainment for the watching crowds.

151 Gladiators fought wild beasts, as well as each other. Fierce wild animals were brought from distant parts of the Roman empire to be killed by gladiators in the arenas in Rome. So many lions were taken from North Africa that they became extinct there.

152 The Colosseum was an amazing building for its time. Also known as the Flavian Amphitheatre, the Colosseum was a huge oval arena in the centre of Rome, used for gladiator fights and mock sea-battles. It opened in AD80, and could seat 50,000 people. It was built of stone, concrete and marble and had 80 separate entrances. Outside, it was decorated with statues of famous Roman heroes.

poles to support
a canopy

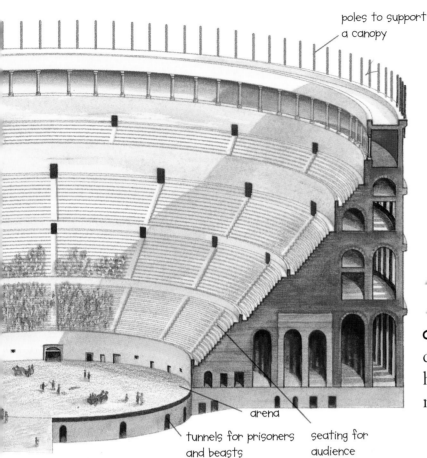

arena

tunnels for prisoners
and beasts

seating for
audience

▲ The Colosseum was the largest
amphitheatre in the Roman empire.

154 **Chariots often collided
and overturned.** Each charioteer
carried a sharp knife, called a 'falx', to cut
himself free from the wreckage. Even so,
many horses and charioteers were killed.

153 **Some Romans preferred a
day at the races.** Horses pulled fast
chariots round race-tracks, called
'circuses'. The most famous was the
Circus Maximus in Rome, which had
room for 250,000 spectators. There could
be up to 24 races each day. Twelve
chariots took part in each race, running
seven times
round the
oval track –
a total
distance of
about eight
kilometres.

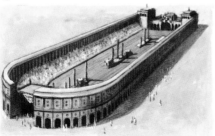

▲ The Circus Maximus

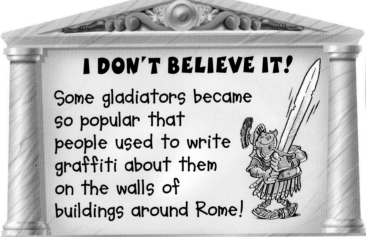

I DON'T BELIEVE IT!

Some gladiators became
so popular that
people used to write
graffiti about them
on the walls of
buildings around Rome!

155 **Racing rivalries could lead
to riots.** Races were organised by four
separate teams – the Reds, Blues, Greens
and Whites. Charioteers wore tunics in
their teams' colours. Each team had a
keen – and violent – group of fans.

73

Ruling Rome

156 Rome used to be ruled by kings. According to legend, the first king was Romulus, who came to power in 753BC. Six more kings ruled after him, but they were unjust and cruel. The last king, Tarquin the Proud, was overthrown in 509BC. After that, Rome became a republic, a state without a king. Every year the people chose two senior lawyers called consuls to head the government. Many other officials were elected, or chosen by the people, too. The republic lasted for over 400 years.

▲ Roman coin showing the emperor Constantine.

▲ Senators were men from leading citizen famili who had served the Roman republic as judges or state officials. They made new laws and discussed government plans.

157 In 47BC a successful general called Julius Caesar declared himself dictator. This meant that he wanted to rule on his own for life. Many people feared that he was trying to end the republic, and rule like the old kings. Caesar was murdered in 44BC by a group of his political enemies. After this, there were many years of civil war.

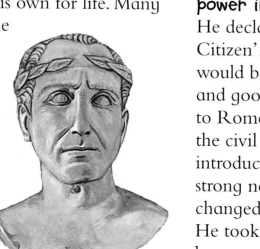

158 In 27BC an army general called Octavian seized power in Rome. He declared himself 'First Citizen', and said he would bring back peace and good government to Rome. He ended the civil war, and introduced many strong new laws. But he also changed the Roman government for ever. He took a new name, 'Augustus' and became the first emperor of Rome.

People could go to the public gallery if there was an interesting case that they wanted to see.

This is a lawyer called an 'advocatus'. These lawyers were called in for serious cases to speak on behalf of the accused person.

▲ The first rules of the Roman legal system were recorded in 450BC in a docment called the Twelve Tables. The Roman system forms the basis of many legal systems today.

If the person accused of the crime refused to go to court, the prosecutor, or person accusing them, could use force to make them go. This could lead to fights.

159 The Romans were proud of their laws. Everyone in Rome, from the emperor to the poorest beggar, was expected to obey the law. Roman laws were strict but fair. Everyone was considered innocent until they had been proved guilty in an open trial.

I DON'T BELIEVE IT!

Some Roman emperors were mad and dangerous. The Emperor Nero was said to have laughed and played music while watching a terrible fire that destroyed a large part of Rome.

In the army

160 **Being a soldier was a good career, if you did not get killed!** Roman soldiers were well paid and well cared for. The empire needed troops to defend its land against enemy attack. A man who fought in the Roman army received a thorough training in battle skills. If he showed promise, he might be promoted and receive extra pay. When he retired after 20 or 25 years' service, he was given money or land to help him start a business.

161 **The Roman army contained citizens and 'helpers'.** Roman citizens joined the regular army, which was organised into legions of around 5,000 men. Men who were not citizens could also fight for Rome. They were known as auxiliaries, or helpers, and were organised in special legions of their own.

162 **Roman troops carried three main weapons.** They fought with javelins, swords and daggers. Each man had to buy his own set. He looked after them carefully – one day, his life might depend on them.

▼ Soldiers used their shields to make a protective shell. It was called a 'testudo', or tortoise.

I DON'T BELIEVE IT!

Roman soldiers guarding the cold northern frontiers of Britain kept warm by wearing short woollen trousers, like underpants, beneath their tunics!

164 **The army advanced 30 kilometres every day.** When they were hurrying to put down a rebellion, or moving from fort to fort, Roman soldiers travelled quickly, on foot. Troops marched along straight, well-made army roads. On the march, each soldier had to carry a heavy pack. It contained weapons, armour, tools for building a camp, cooking pots, dried food and spare clothes.

163 **Soldiers needed many skills.** In enemy territory, soldiers had to find or make everything they needed to survive. When they first arrived they built camps of tents, but soon afterwards they built permanent forts defended by strong walls. Each legion contained men with a wide range of skills, such as cooks, builders, carpenters, doctors, blacksmiths and engineers – but they all had to fight!

165 **Soldiers worshipped their own special god.** At forts and army camps, Roman soldiers built temples where they honoured Mithras, their own god. They believed he protected them, and gave them life after death.

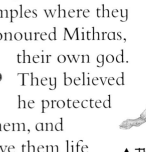

▲ The Roman god Mithras wrestles with a bull.

barracks, where soldiers sleep

exercise yard

gate

protective wall

Ruled by Rome

166 Over 50 million people were ruled by Rome. Celts, Germans, Iberians, Dacians and many other peoples lived in territory conquered by Roman armies. They spoke many different languages, and had different customs and beliefs. Roman rulers sent armies to occupy their lands, and governors to rule them. They forced conquered peoples to pay Roman taxes and obey Roman laws.

▲ A Roman tax collector assesses a farmer for taxes.

167 A few conquered kings and queens refused to accept Roman rule. For example, in AD60 Boudicca, queen of the Iceni tribe who lived in eastern England, led a rebellion against the Romans in Britain. Her army marched on the city of London and set fire to it, before being defeated by Roman soldiers. Boudicca survived the battle, but killed herself by taking poison so that she would not be captured by Roman troops.

168 Cleopatra used beauty and charm to stop the Romans invading. Cleopatra was queen of Egypt, in North Africa. Cleopatra knew that the Egyptian army would not be able to defeat Roman soldiers. Two Roman army generals, Julius Caesar and Mark Antony, fell in love with her. She stopped the Romans invading for many years, but Egypt was eventually conquered.

▼ A carving from Trajan's column of Roman legionaries boarding ships.

169 **Roman conquerors built monuments to celebrate their victories.** Trajan, who ruled from AD98–117, was a famous soldier who became emperor of Rome. He led Roman armies on one of their most successful conquests, in Dacia (Romania) in AD106. To record this achievement, he gave orders for a tall stone pillar (now known as Trajan's Column) to be built in the Forum in Rome. It was almost 30 metres high, and was decorated with carvings of 2,500 Roman soldiers winning wars.

▲ Trajan's column

PAINT YOURSELF LIKE A CELTIC WARRIOR!

Roman writers reported how Celtic warriors decorated their faces and bodies with patterns before going into battle. They believed that the paint was magic, and would protect them. The Celts used a deep blue dye made from a plant called woad. If you have some special face-painting make-up (make sure you ask an adult), then try making up some scary war-paint designs of your own!

▲ A carving from Trajan's column of Roman soldiers building the walls of a new fort.

The farming life

170 Rome relied on farmers. Most people in Roman times lived in the countryside and worked on farms. Farmers produced food for city-dwellers. Without them, the citizens would not have survived. Food was grown on big estates by teams of slaves, and on small peasant farms where single families worked together.

171 Farm produce was imported from all over the empire. Wool and honey came from Britain, wine came from Greece, and 400,000 tonnes of wheat were shipped across the Mediterranean Sea from Egypt every year. It was ground into flour, which was used to make bread, the Romans' staple, or basic, food.

172 Farmers had no machines to help them. Heavy work was done by animals, or by human muscle-power. Ploughs were pulled by oxen. Ripe crops were harvested by men and women with curved knives called sickles, and loaded by hand onto farm carts. Donkeys turned mill wheels to crush olives and grind grain, and to raise drinking water from wells.

beehives for honey

treading grapes for wine

owner of the farm

threshing wheat

sheep kept in the fields

pressing olives

vegetable patch

farmworkers harvesting grain

vineyard and orchard

174 **The most valuable fruit was small, hard, green and bitter!** It came from olive trees. Olives could be pickled in salty water to eat with bread and cheese, or crushed to provide oil. The Romans used olive oil as a medicine, for cooking and preserving food, for cleaning and softening the skin, and even for burning in lamps.

173 **Roman grapes grew on trees!** Vines, climbing plants that produce grapes, were planted among fruit trees in Roman orchards. They provided support for the vine stems, and welcome shade to stop the grapes getting scorched by the sun. Grapes were one of the most important crops on Roman farms. The ripe fruits were picked and dried to become raisins, or pulped and made into wine.

QUIZ

Imagine that you are a Roman farmer, talking to a visitor from the city. How would you answer their questions:

What crops do you grow?
Why do you keep oxen?
Who will harvest that grain?
How do you grind grain into flour?
Why are you growing olives?

Work like a slave!

175 Roman people were not all equal. There were different classes within Roman society. Throughout the Roman empire, the biggest difference between people was whether they were slaves or free. Free-born men and women had rights that were guaranteed by law, for example, to find their own work, or travel from one place to another. In Rome, citizens also had the right to vote for government officials, and to receive free hand-outs of food. But slaves had hardly any rights at all. They belonged to their owners just like dogs or horses.

176 Slaves were trained to do all sorts of tasks. Slaves did everything their owners demanded, from babycare to hard labour on farms. Many slaves were trusted by their owners, who valued their skills. A few slaves became respected chefs or doctors.

▼ Slaves were bought and sold at slave-markets like this one. They could not leave, or choose what work to do. They could be cruelly punished, neglected, or given away.

177 There were many different ways of becoming a slave. Slaves might be captured in war, purchased from a slave-trader or born to slave parents. They could also be people condemned to slavery as punishment for a serious crime.

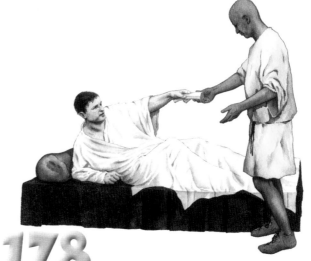

Slaves were paraded before the citizens to be chosen or rejected.

178 Slaves were sometimes set free by their owners. Freedom could be a reward for loyalty or long service. Some sick or dying slave-owners gave orders that their slaves should be freed. They did not want their slaves to pass to a new owner who might treat them badly.

I DON'T BELIEVE IT!

From 73BC to 71BC a slave called Spartacus led a revolt in southern Italy. He ran away to a hideout in the hills where 90,000 other slaves joined him.

179 Some slaves did very well after they were freed. Former slaves used the skills they had learned to set up businesses of their own. Many were successful, and a few became very rich.

Roman know-how

180 The Romans pioneered many new building materials and designs. They discovered concrete, which was much cheaper and easier to use than stone. They made bricks of clay baked at high temperatures which lasted much longer than unbaked ones. They found out how to use arches to create tall, strong walls and doorways. They designed massive domes for buildings that were too big to be roofed with wooden beams.

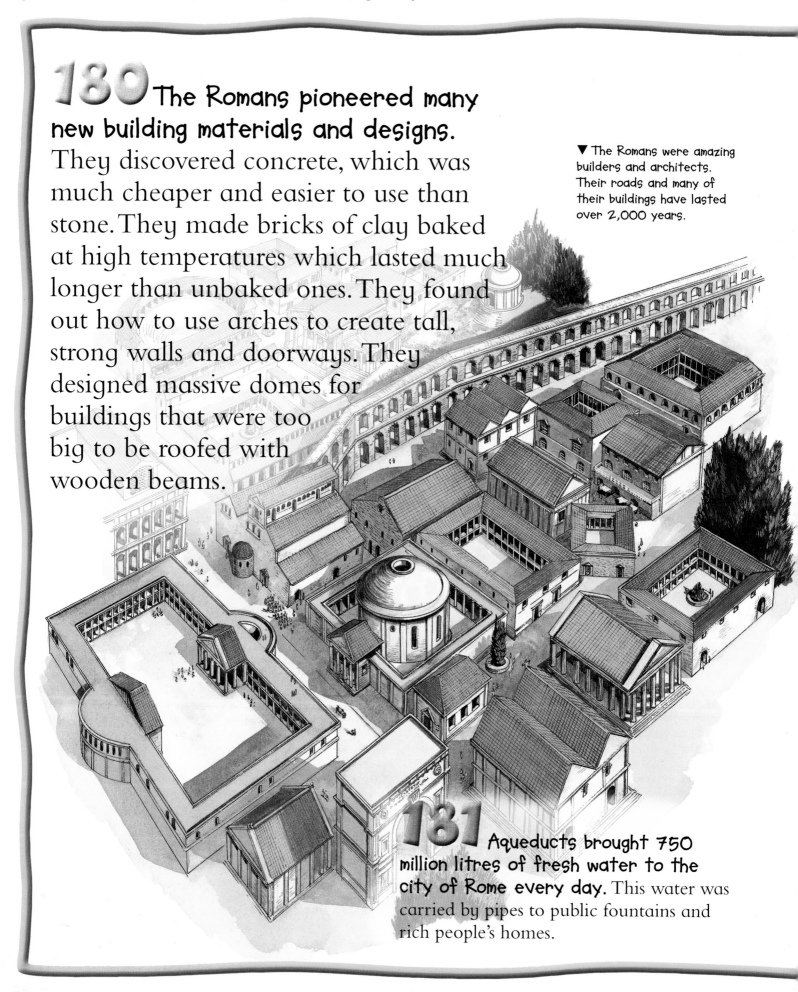

▼ The Romans were amazing builders and architects. Their roads and many of their buildings have lasted over 2,000 years.

181 Aqueducts brought 750 million litres of fresh water to the city of Rome every day. This water was carried by pipes to public fountains and rich people's homes.

▲ This is a Roman valve that allowed water to be pumped uphill. Water would then come out of fountains such as the one shown here.

182 Roman water supplies were so advanced that no one had anything better until the 1800s! They invented pumps with valves to pump water uphill. This went into high tanks above fountains. Gravity pulled the water out of the fountain's spout.

184 Even the best doctors often failed to cure their patients. But Roman doctors were skilled at sewing up cuts and joining broken bones. They also used herbs for medicines and painkillers.

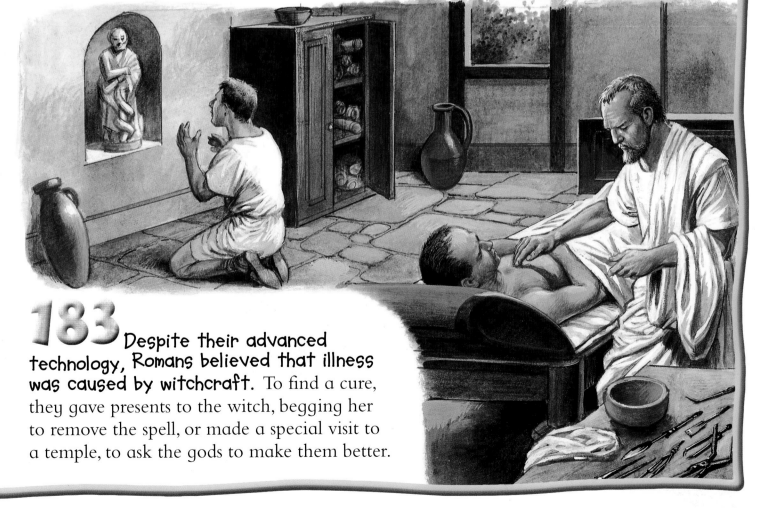

183 Despite their advanced technology, Romans believed that illness was caused by witchcraft. To find a cure, they gave presents to the witch, begging her to remove the spell, or made a special visit to a temple, to ask the gods to make them better.

Prayers and sacrifices

185 The Romans worshipped many different gods. Jupiter, the king of the gods, protected Roman lands. His wife Juno was worshipped by married women. Mars was the god of war, Venus was the goddess of love. Diana, the moon goddess, guarded young girls and wild animals; Neptune, god of the sea, sent earthquakes and terrible storms. Vesta was the goddess of Roman homes. Her priestesses tended a holy flame in a temple in the Forum in Rome.

Jupiter, king of the gods

Juno, queen of the gods

Mercury, the messenger of the gods

Neptune, god of the sea

Mars

Venus, goddess of love

Minerva goddess of war

Diana, goddess of the moon and hunting

Pan, god of the mountainside, pastures, sheep and goats

Dis (Pluto) god of the underworld

186 The Roman emperor was also chief priest. As part of his government duties he said prayers and offered sacrifices to the gods who protected Rome. He was given a special name 'pontifex maximus' which meant chief bridge-builder, because people believed he acted as a bridge between the gods and ordinary people.

187
Families made offerings to the gods every day. They left food, wine and incense in front of a shrine in their house. A shrine is like a mini church. It contained statues of ancient gods called the 'lares' and 'penates'. The lares were ancestor spirits, who looked after living family members. The penates guarded the family's food.

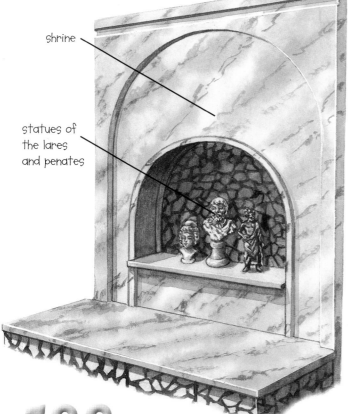

shrine

statues of the lares and penates

188
Roman people were very superstitious. They decorated their homes with magic symbols, and hung good luck charms round children's necks. They believed that they could foretell the future by observing animals, birds, insects and even the weather! For example, bees were a sign of riches and happiness but a hooting owl foretold danger.

189
Roman men and women could ask the gods to curse their enemies. They wrote their enemies' names, plus curse words, on scraps of metal or pottery and left them at temples. They hoped that the gods would see these messages, and harm the people named in them.

190
Some of the world's first Christians lived in Rome. But until AD313 Christianity was banned in the Roman Empire. Christians met secretly, in underground passages called catacombs, to say prayers and hold services. They also used the catacombs as a burial place.

I DON'T BELIEVE IT!
After an animal had been sacrificed to the gods, a priest, called a 'haruspex', examined its liver. If it was diseased, bad luck was on the way!

On the move

191 **All roads led to Rome.** The city was at the hub of a network of roads that stretched for over 85,000 kilometres. They had been built to link outlying parts of the empire to the capital, so that Roman armies or government officials could travel quickly. To make travel as quick as possible, roads were built in straight lines, taking the shortest route.

▲ This map shows the Roman Empire in brown, and the roads that they built in black.

192 **Rome's first main road was built in 312BC.** Its name was the Via Appia ('via' is the Latin word for road), and it ran from the city of Rome to the port of Brundisium on the south-east coast of Italy. Many travellers from Greece arrived there, and the new road made their journey to Rome quicker and easier.

193 **Some Roman roads have survived for over 2,000 years!** Each road was made of layers of earth and stones on top of a firm, flat foundation. It was surfaced with stone slabs or gravel. The centre had a camber, a curved surface, so that rainwater drained away into ditches on either side.

large surface slabs

drainage ditch

solid foundations

route accurately marked out

194
Roman engineers used tools to help them make accurate surveys. They made careful plans and took measurements before starting any big building project, such as a new road or city walls.

▲ These road builders are using a 'groma' to measure straight lines.

195
Poor people had to walk everywhere. They could not afford to hire a horse or a donkey, or a cushioned carriage, pulled by oxen. If they were lucky, they might manage to hitch a lift in a lumbering farm wagon – but this would not give them a comfortable ride!

196
Town streets were crowded and very dirty. Rich people travelled in curtained beds called litters, carried shoulder-high by slaves. Ordinary people used stepping-stones to avoid the mud and rubbish underfoot.

197
Heavy loads often travelled by water. There were no big lorries in Roman times! Ships powered by sails and by slaves rowing carried people and cargo across the sea and along rivers. But water-transport was slow, and could be dangerous. Roman ships were often attacked by pirates, and shipwrecks were common.

▲ The Romans' knowledge of ship-building, as in this trading ship came from the Greeks. The Romans, though, were not really sailors, and they did not improve the designs.

Digging up Rome

198 Large amounts of evidence survives to tell us about Roman times. Archaeologists have discovered the remains of many Roman buildings throughout Roman empire lands, including palaces, forts, walls, aqueducts, temples, hospitals, theatres and ordinary family homes. They have also found Roman works of art, together with glittering gold and silver coins, beautiful jewellery, fine pottery and delicate glass, and many tools and household objects used by Roman men and women in their daily lives.

Intricate Roman mosaic

These are lamps that burned olive oil for light.

Statues can give us an idea what the Romans looked like.

199 We can still see many Roman designs today. Until the 20th century, grand, important buildings were often planned and decorated in Roman style. Architects believed that Roman designs inspired respect in anyone who saw them. For this reason, many big cities in Europe, America and elsewhere have churches, museums, art-galleries, colleges and even banks that look like Roman temples or Roman villas.

Roman pots

QUIZ
1. Who was the king of the Roman gods?
2. What is the proper name for a mini church in someone's house?
3. When was Rome's first road built?
4. What is the proper name for a curtained bed?

1. Jupiter 2. A shrine 3. 312BC 4. A litter

Roman people liked intricate and expensive jewellery.

Roman coins show the most important people of the time, often the emperor.

200 Many people still have Roman names. In many parts of the world, parents still like to give their children Roman names, or names based on Latin words. Here are some popular ones: Amanda (Loveable), Diana (Moon Goddess), Venus (Goddess of Love), Patricia (Noble), Laura (Laurel-tree), Virginia (Maiden), Julius (Roman family name), Antony (Roman family name), Martin (God of War), Marcus (God of War), Victor (Winner), Vincent (Conqueror).

▲ An archaeologist's dig uncovers remains from the Roman period. Their finds give us a better understanding of how the Romans lived.

Castle life

201 **A castle was both a home and a fortress in the Middle Ages.** It provided shelter for a king or a lord and his family, and it allowed him to defend his lands. Castles were also places where soldiers were stationed, wrong-doers were imprisoned, courts settled disputes, weapons and armour were made and great banquets and tournaments were held.

In the beginning

202 The first castles were mostly built from wood on top of a hill. Sometimes castle builders piled up soil to make the hill artificially. On top of the hill, called a motte, stood a wooden tower, or keep. This was the central part of the castle and the easiest part to defend.

▼ This is a motte and bailey castle. The Normans from France introduced this kind of castle in the 1000s, and it soon became popular across Europe.

◀ Castles and forts have been built all over the world since the earliest times. This is the fortified town of Great Zimbabwe, in modern day Zimbabwe. The oldest part dates from the 700s.

▶ By the 1500s the Japanese were building strong, permanent castles of their own. Castles were often built with different layers to fire on the enemy from different heights.

203 At the bottom of the motte was a courtyard that was called a bailey. It was usually surrounded by a wooden fence. Castle builders dug a deep ditch, called a moat, all around the outside of the motte and bailey. They often filled the moat with water. Moats were designed to stop attackers reaching the castle walls.

◀ For extra protection, a wooden fence was often built around the top of the motte. The top of each wooden plank was shaped into a point to make it harder for the enemy to climb over.

204 Wooden castles were not very strong – and they caught fire easily. From around 1100 onwards, people began to build castles in stone. A stone castle gave better protection against attack, fire and cold rainy weather.

gatehouse

inner defensive wall

outer defensive wall

keep

turret

▶ Sometimes an extra wall was built on the inside of the strong outer wall. Archers could stand on the inner wall and fire down onto the outer wall if it was captured.

Building a castle

205 **The best place to build a castle was on top of a hill.** A hilltop position gave good views over the surrounding countryside, and made it harder for an enemy to launch a surprise attack. Sometimes a castle was built on the banks of a river or lake, and its waters were used to create a moat.

206

The lord of the castle and his family lived in the safest part of the castle – the keep.
The walls of the keep were built to be very strong, and at least 3.5 metres thick in some castles. Inside the keep were large rooms for receiving visitors and holding banquets, as well as smaller storerooms and guardrooms. The family's bedrooms were on the top floor of the keep. All these rooms and defences made building a castle very slow and expensive.

DESIGN YOUR OWN CASTLE

Imagine you have been asked to design a castle for your local lord. It is very important that he can defend his castle and his family against attacks by his enemies.

Draw a plan of your ideal castle, making sure it has plenty of defences. And don't forget the drawbridge to let the lord and his family in and out of their castle stronghold.

Who's who in the castle

207 A castle was the home of an important and powerful person, such as a king, a lord or a knight. The lord of the castle controlled the castle itself, as well as the lands and people around it. The lady of the castle was in charge of the day-to-day running of the castle. She controlled the kitchens and gave the servants their orders for feasts and banquets.

▶ Lord and lady of the manor

208 The constable was in charge of defending the castle. He trained his soldiers to guard the castle properly and organized the rota of guards and watchmen. The constable was in charge of the whole castle when the lord was away.

209 Many servants lived and worked inside the castle, looking after the lord and his family. They cooked, cleaned, served at table, worked as maids and servants and ran errands. A man called the steward was in charge of all the servants.

Servants   Steward   Cooks

210 Inside the castle walls were many workshops where goods were made and repaired. The castle blacksmith was kept busy making shoes for all the horses. The armourer made weapons and armour.

Armourer

Blacksmith

▶ The master of the horse had to look after the lord's horses.

211 Local villagers would shelter in the castle when their lands were under attack. They were not allowed to shelter inside the keep itself, so they stayed inside the bailey with their families and all their animals.

From kings to peasants

212 In medieval times, the king or queen was the most important person in the country. The king gave land to his barons and other noblemen. In return, they supplied the king with soldiers, horses and weapons to fight wars. This system of giving away land in return for services was known as feudalism.

▶ This bishop is having a meeting, called an audience, with the king and queen. In medieval times there was often conflict between the Church and the king. Both were very powerful, and they had to try to work together.

213 The Church was very powerful at this time. It controlled large areas of land, and grew rich from the taxes paid by the peasants who worked on these lands. Peasant farmers had to give the church a tithe, one-tenth of everything they produced.

214 The barons were the most powerful noblemen. A wealthy baron might supply the king with around 5,000 fighting men. Some barons also had their own private army to keep control over their own lands.

215 The wealthier lords and barons often gave away some of their lands to professional fighters called knights. Knights were skilled soldiers who rode into battle on horseback.

Quiz

1. What is the name of the mound of soil on which early castles were built?
2. Which was the safest and best-protected part of the castle?
3. What is a moat?
4. Who was in charge of the castle guards?
5. What did the king give to his lords in return for their services?

1. a motte 2. the keep 3. a water-filled ditch around the outside of the castle walls 4. the constable 5. land

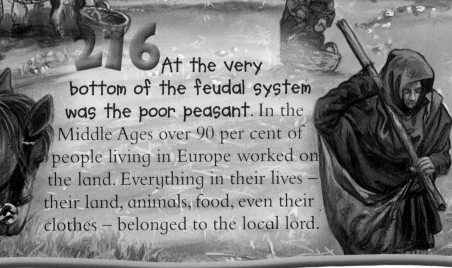

216 At the very bottom of the feudal system was the poor peasant. In the Middle Ages over 90 per cent of people living in Europe worked on the land. Everything in their lives — their land, animals, food, even their clothes — belonged to the local lord.

How to be a good knight

217 *It took about 14 years of training to become a knight.* The son of a noble joined a lord's household aged seven. He learned how to ride, to shoot a bow and arrow and how to behave in front of nobles. He then became a squire, where he learned how to fight with a sword, and he looked after his master's armour and weapons. If he was successful, he became a knight at 21.

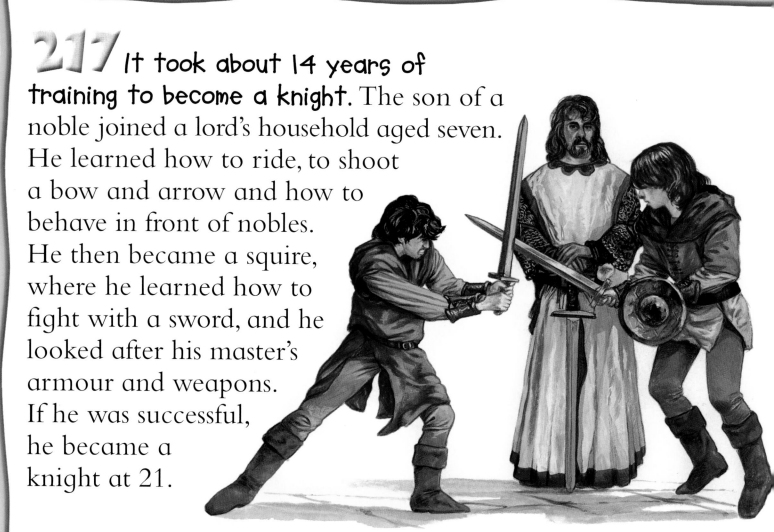

218 *The ceremony of making a new knight was known as dubbing.* A knight had to spend a whole night in church before his dubbing ceremony took place. This all-night watch was called a vigil. First, he had a cold bath and dressed in a plain white tunic. Then he spent the night on his knees in church, praying and confessing his sins.

219

The dubbing ceremony changed over time. In the beginning a knight was struck on the back of the neck. Later, dubbing involved a tap on the knight's shoulder with a sword.

220

Knights had to behave according to a set of rules, known as the 'code of chivalry'. The code involved being brave and honourable on the battlefield, and treating the enemy politely and fairly. It also instructed knights how to behave towards women.

221

A knight who behaved badly was disgraced and punished. A knight in disgrace had either behaved in a cowardly way on the battlefield, cheated in a tournament or treated another knight badly.

222

A rich knight would have three horses. He rode his heaviest horse for fighting and tournaments. He also had a horse for riding, and a baggage horse. The best horses were warhorses from Italy and Spain. They were quick but strong and sturdy.

Ready for battle

223 Knights wore a long-sleeved tunic made of linen or wool, with a cloak over the top. By the 1200s knights had started to wear long hooded coats called surcoats. Knights nearly always wore bright colours, and some even wore fancy items such as shoes with curled pointed toes, and hats decorated with sparkling jewels.

◀ A knight was dressed for battle from the feet upwards. The last item of armour to be put on him was his helmet.

224 Early knights wore a type of armour called chainmail. It was made of thousands of tiny iron rings joined onto each other. A piece of chainmail looked a bit like knitting, except it was made of metal, not wool. But a a knight also wore a padded jacket under his chainmail to make sure he wasn't cut by his own armour!

225 Gradually, knights began to wear more and more armour. They added solid metal plates shaped to fit their body. By the 1400s knights were wearing full suits of steel armour. They wore metal gloves, called gauntlets, and even metal shoes!

226 A knight had two main weapons: his sword and his shield. The sword was double edged and was sharp enough to pierce chainmail. Knights also fought with lances, daggers and axes.

◀ These knights are fighting in battle. The knight on the right has the usual weapons of a sword and shield. The knight on the left has a morning star. This was a spiked ball on the end of a chain.

227 Between 1337 and 1453 England and France were almost continually at war with each other, what we now know as the Hundred Years' War. The English armies won important battles against the French in 1356 and at Agincourt in 1415. The skilled English and Welsh longbowmen, who could fire as many as 12 arrows every minute, helped to stop the French knights.

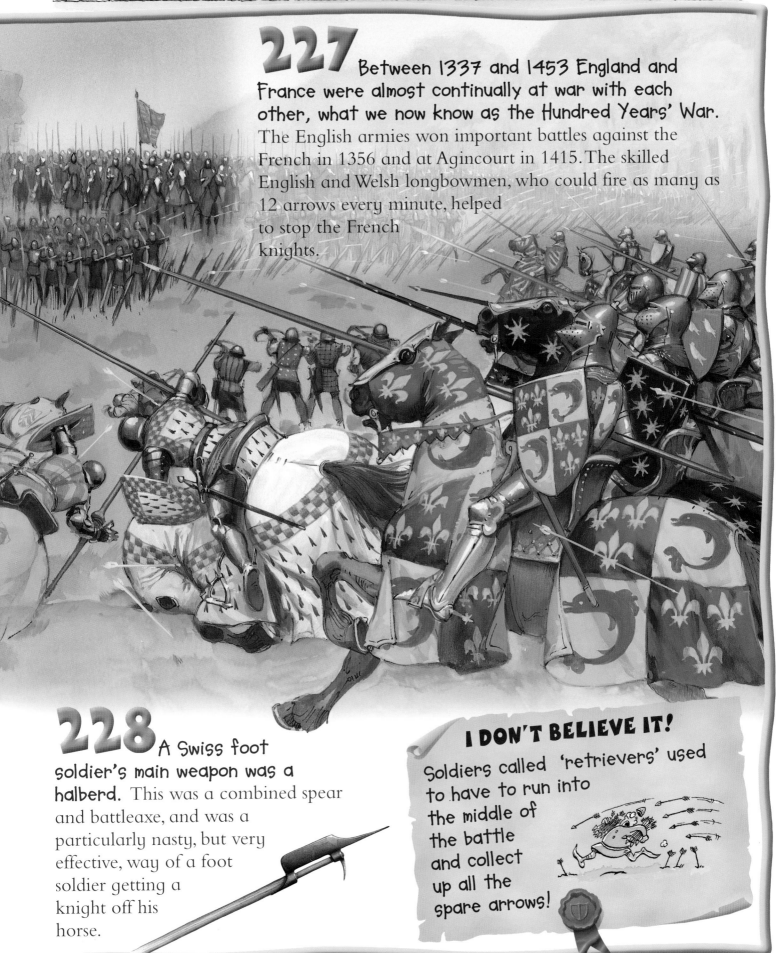

228 A Swiss foot soldier's main weapon was a halberd. This was a combined spear and battleaxe, and was a particularly nasty, but very effective, way of a foot soldier getting a knight off his horse.

I DON'T BELIEVE IT!

Soldiers called 'retrievers' used to have to run into the middle of the battle and collect up all the spare arrows!

Colours and coats of arms

229 When a knight went into battle in full armour wearing a helmet with a visor, no one could recognize him. This problem was solved by putting a different set of coloured symbols on each knight's shield. These sets of symbols became known as coats of arms, and each family had its own personal design. No other family was allowed to use that design.

Heraldry, the system of using coats of arms, became a very complex system of signs and symbols. Schools of heraldry were set up to sort out disputes over coats of arms.

230 Only certain colours and styles of design could be used to create a coat of arms. The colours allowed were red, blue, black, green, purple, silver and gold. The arms also indicated the wearer's position in his family. So, a second son showed a crescent symbol, and a seventh son displayed a rose.

231 On the battlefield, each nobleman had his own banner around which his knights and other soldiers could meet. The nobleman's colours and coat of arms were displayed on the banner. Banners decorated with coats of arms also made a colourful display at tournaments and parades.

◄ The banner of a nobleman was a very important symbol during battle. If the person holding the banner was killed in battle, someone had to pick the banner up and raise it straight away.

232

Messengers called heralds carried messages between knights during battle. They had to be able to recognize each individual knight quickly. After coats of arms were introduced, the heralds became experts at identifying them. The system of using coats of arms became known as heraldry.

▲ After a battle, it was the sad job of a herald to walk around the battlefield and identify the dead by their coats of arms.

DESIGN YOUR OWN COAT OF ARMS

Would you like your own personal coat of arms? You can design one by following the basic rules of heraldry explained on these pages. You will need the seven paint colours listed opposite, a paintbrush, a fine-tipped black felt pen, a ruler and some thick white paper. Good luck!

Famous knights

233 Roland was a brave, loyal knight who died in the service of his master. Roland served King Charles the Great – Charlemagne – who ruled much of France and Germany in the 800s. Roland had to protect Charlemagne and his army from Muslim attackers as they crossed from Spain into France. But Roland was betrayed and died fighting for his king.

▲ Famous stories of old knights have been recorded in old books, like this one bound in leather.

234 The Spanish knight Rodrigo Díaz de Vivar had the nickname 'El Cid'. This comes from the Arabic for 'the Lord'. El Cid fought against the Moors from North Africa. He was exiled by his lord, King Alfonso VI, after the knight's enemies turned the king against him.

▼ Don Quixote charged at windmills because he thought they were giants.

▲ Rodrigo Díaz de Vivar, 'El Cid'

235 The book 'Don Quixote' tells the story of an old man who dreams about past deeds of bravery and chivalry. It was written in the 1500s by a Spaniard called Miguel de Cervantes. After reading about the knights of old, Don Quixote dresses in armour and sets off to become famous. He takes a peasant called Sancho Panzo with him as his squire, and it is his squire who gets Don Quixote out of trouble during his travels.

236

Lancelot was the favourite knight of King Arthur. Tales of Arthur and his Knights of the Round Table were very popular in the 1200s. Lancelot fell in love with Arthur's wife Guinevere. The struggle between the two men, and the scandal caused by the romance between Lancelot and Guinevere, eventually destroyed Arthur's court.

237

The Black Prince was the nickname of Edward, the oldest son of Edward III of England. The Black Prince was a great warrior who captured the French king, John II, at the battle of Poitiers in 1356.

I DON'T BELIEVE IT!

During his travels Don Quixote mistakes flocks of farmyard animals for enemy armies!

A castle tour

238 Stone castles were cold damp places with lots of draughts. A castle was not exactly a luxury home. Cold winds blew through the windows, which had no glass.

▶ The lord of the castle and his family were the only people who slept in beds. Most people slept on wooden pallets covered with straw.

Quiz

1. Which were the two main battle weapons of a knight?

2. Why did knights start to display a coat of arms?

3. Who was Sir Lancelot?

4. Who was the Black Prince?

5. What was the name of the castle toilet?

▶ Almost all castles also had a well, within their walls. This was essential as a source of water if someone laid siege to the castle.

▶ The kitchens were often built in a separate part of the castle, away from the keep, in case they caught fire.

1. a sword and a shield 2. to be recognized on the battlefield 3. the favourite knight of King Arthur 4. Prince Edward, the son of Edward III 5. the garderobe

▼ Castles had no central heating and no running water. Wool hangings and tapestries on the walls, and rugs on the floor, helped to warm the rooms. Roaring fires burned in the huge fireplaces.

239 There were many workshops and other buildings inside the safety of the castle walls. They included an armoury, a smithy, stables, kennels, a mill for making flour and a chapel. There were sometimes even gardens and orchards!

240 Medieval castles had no toilets! Instead people sat on wooden seats called 'garderobes'. These were built over a very long chute. Waste from the toilet fell down the chute into the moat.

◀ Every castle had a cold, dark and often slimy dungeon for keeping prisoners. The dungeon was usually located beneath one of the gatehouse towers. Prisoners would be locked inside a small airless cell.

Feasts and fun

241 The Great Hall was the centre of castle life. The lord and his family ate their meals here and carried out their daily business. Colourful banners and coats of arms and shiny pieces of armour hung from the walls of the Great Hall. The hall was sometimes turned into a courtroom.

242 Musicians entertained the lord and his guests at banquets in the Great Hall. They played instruments such as pipes, drums, fiddles and lutes.

243 Jesters, jugglers and acrobats performed for the diners between courses. Sometimes a dancing bear might be brought in to entertain the guests.

BAKE A 'TARTE OF APPLES AND ORANGES'

You will need:
a packet of
shortcrust pastry
4 eating apples
4 oranges
juice of ½ lemon
3 cups of water
1 cup of honey
½ cup of
brown sugar
¼ tsp cinnamon
a pinch of
dried ginger
a little milk
a little caster sugar

Ask an adult to help you. Line a pie dish with pastry and bake for 10 minutes in a medium-hot oven. Slice the oranges thinly. Boil the water, honey and lemon juice, add the oranges. Cover and simmer for 2 hours, then drain. Peel, core and slice the apples and mix with the sugar, cinnamon and ginger. Place a layer of apples in the bottom of the dish followed by a layer of oranges, then alternate layers until the fruit is used up. Place a pastry lid over the top and brush with a little milk. Make small slits in the lid. Bake in a medium-hot oven for about 45 minutes.

244 Huge amounts of exotic-looking and delicious foods were served at banquets. Roast meats included stuffed peacock and swan, as well as venison, beef, goose, duck and wild boar. Whole roasted fish were also served. These foods were followed by dishes made from spices brought from Asia, and then fruit and nuts.

245 The lord, his family and important guests sat at the high table on a platform called a dais. From their raised position they could look down over the rest of the diners. The most important guests such as priests and noblemen sat next to the lord.

246 Important guests drank fine wine out of proper glasses. Cup-bearers poured the wine out of decorated pottery jugs. Less important diners drank ale or wine from mugs or tankards made of wood, pewter or leather.

Songs, poems and love

247 Medieval minstrels sang songs and recited poetry about love and bravery. These songs and poems showed knights as faithful, loving and religious men who were prepared to die for their king or lard. A true knight fought for justice and fairness for everyone. In real life, knights did not always live up to this ideal picture.

◀ Minstrels sang their songs to the accompaniment of sweet-sounding music from a harp or lute.

▼ Knights offered to perform brave and heroic acts at tournaments to prove the strength of their love.

248 A style of romantic behaviour called courtly love was popular among knights in both France and England. It was a kind of false love carried out by following strict rules. Courtly love stated that a knight had to fall in love with a woman of equal or higher rank – and ideally she should be married to someone else. Their love had to be kept secret.

249

Troubadours were poet–musicians who composed songs about heroic knights and ideal love. They lived in France in the 1100s and 1200s. Some troubadours had themselves been knights at one time, and they told rather exaggerated stories of their own deeds of love and bravery.

▲ Richard I of England, who is better known as Richard the Lionheart, was a troubadour. Some of the songs he wrote have been preserved.

250

A knight wrote secret letters to the woman he loved. He had to worship his loved one from a distance, and could never declare his love for a lady directly to her.

▶ A knight and his love wrote poems to each other, expressing their feelings of love and devotion.

ILLUMINATED LETTERS

The first letter of a manuscript, called an illuminated letter, was much larger than the others, and it was decorated with pictures and patterns.

You can create your own set of illuminated letters for the initials of your name. Draw the outline of the letter in fine black pen and then use felt-tipped pens or paints to add the decoration.

▶ An illuminated letter 'C'.

Knights and dragons

251 The legend of St George tells how the brave knight killed a fierce white dragon. The dragon was terrorizing the people of Lydia (part of modern Turkey). The king offered his daughter to the dragon if the dragon left his people alone. St George arrived and said he would kill their dragon if they became Christians like him. Thousands accepted his offer, and George killed the dragon.

▲ St George was adopted as the patron saint of England in the 1300s.

252 Ivanhoe was a medieval knight who lived in the time of Richard the Lionheart. He is the hero of a historical book called 'Ivanhoe', written by the Scottish novelist Sir Walter Scott in the 1800s. 'Ivanhoe' describes the conflict between the Saxon people and their Norman conquerors at a time when the Normans had ruled England for at least 100 years.

253 Legend says that King Arthur became king after pulling a magic sword called Excalibur out of a stone. This act proved that he was the right person to rule Britain. People have written stories about Arthur and his followers, the Knights of the Round Table, for more than 1,000 years.

◀ No one really knows who the real Arthur was, but he may have been a Celtic warrior who lived about 1,400 years ago.

255 In the 1300s an Englishman called Geoffrey Chaucer wrote 'The Canterbury Tales'. These stories were about a group of pilgrims travelling from London to a religious site in Canterbury. The pilgrims included a priest, a nun, a merchant, a cook, a ploughman and a knight and his squire.

254 King Arthur had many castle homes but his favourite was Camelot. Historians think that Camelot was really an English castle called Tintagel. When Arthur heard that his best friend and favourite knight, Sir Lancelot, had fallen in love with Arthur's wife, Queen Guinevere, Arthur banished Lancelot from his court at Camelot.

Quiz

1. What is a minstrel?

2. Whose job was it to fill everyone's glass at a banquet?

3. What did a troubadour do?

4. Who were the Knights of the Round Table?

5. What is the name of King Arthur's favourite castle?

1. a wandering musician 2. the cup-bearer 3. write songs about knights and courtly love 4. the followers of King Arthur 5. Camelot

Practice for battle

256 In a tournament, knights divided into two sides and fought each other as if in a proper battle. Tournaments were good practice for the real thing – war. The idea for these mock battles, called tourneys, probably started in France in the 12th century.

▲ Edward I of England was a keen supporter of tournaments and jousts. He banned spectators from carrying weapons themselves because this caused too much trouble among the watching crowds.

▼ Jousting knights charged at each other at top speed. Each one tried to knock his opponent off his horse with a blow from a long wooden lance.

257 Tournaments took place under strict rules. There were safe areas where knights could rest without being attacked by the other side. Knights were not meant to kill their opponents but they often did. Several kings became so angry at losing their best knights that all tournaments were banned unless the king had given his permission.

258 Jousting was introduced because so many knights were being killed or wounded during tournaments. More than 60 knights were killed in a single tourney in Cologne, Germany. Jousting was a fight between two knights on horseback. Each knight tried to win by knocking the other off his horse. Knights were protected by armour, and their lances were not sharp.

259 A knight's code of chivalry did not allow him to win a tournament by cheating. It was better to lose with honour than to win in disgrace.

I DON'T BELIEVE IT!

Some knights cheated in jousts by wearing special armour that was fixed onto the horse's saddle!

260 Sometimes the knights carried on fighting on the ground with their swords. The problem was that this was as dangerous as a tourney!

261 A joust gave a knight the chance to prove himself in front of the woman he loved. Jousts were very social events watched by ladies of the court as well as ordinary people. Knights could show off their skills and bravery to impress the spectators.

Friend or enemy?

262 When Edward the Confessor died in 1066, Duke William of Normandy, his cousin, claimed that he had been promised the throne of England. William and his knights invaded England and defeated Harold, the English king, at the Battle of Hastings.

▲ The Bayeux Tapestry records the story of the Norman invasion of England. It shows William and his knights landing along the English coast, and also shows the moment when England's King Harold was killed at the Battle of Hastings.

▲ Here you can see the route that William the Conqueror took to London.

263 On and off between 1337 and 1453 the neighbouring countries of England and France were at war. The Hundred Years' War, as it was called, carried on through the reigns of five English kings and five French ones. The two countries fought each other to decide who should control France. In the end the French were victorious, and England lost control of all her lands in France apart from the port of Calais.

264 One of the major battles of the Hundred Years' War was fought at Crécy in 1346. English soldiers defeated a much larger French army, killing almost half the French soldiers. During the battle, the English army used gunpowder and cannons for possibly the first time.

265 Deadly weapons called caltrops were used in the Hundred Years' War. A caltrop was a star-shaped piece of metal. These were scattered along the ground in front of an attacking army. They stopped both horses and footsoldiers in their tracks.

266 A young French girl called Joan of Arc led the French army against the English, who had surrounded the city of Orléans. After 10 days the English were defeated. Joan was later captured, accused of being a witch, and burned to death.

I DON'T BELIEVE IT!
If you captured a knight alive during battle, you could offer him back to his family in return for a generous ransom!

Under attack

267 An attacking enemy had to break through a castle's defences to get inside its walls. One method was to break down the castle gates with giant battering rams. Attackers and defenders also used siege engines to hurl boulders at each other.

268 A siege is when an enemy surrounds a castle and stops all supplies from reaching the people inside. The idea is to starve the castle occupants until they surrender or die.

269 A riskier way of trying to get inside a castle was to climb over the walls. Attackers either used ladders or moved wooden towers with men hidden inside them into position beside the walls.

270 Giant catapults were sometimes uses to fire stones or burning pieces of wood inside the castle. The Romans were some of the first people to use catapults in warfare.

▶ Attackers could also dig a tunnel under a wall or a tower. They would then light a fire that burnt away the tunnel's supports. The tunnel collapsed, and brought down the building above.

▲ This siege engine was called a trebuchet. It had a long wooden arm with a heavy weight at one end and a sling at the other. A heavy stone was placed inside the sling. As the weight dropped, the stone was hurled towards the castle walls, sometimes travelling as far as 300 metres.

271 The enemy sometimes succeeded in tunnelling beneath the castle walls. They surprised the defenders when they appeared inside the castle itself.

I DON'T BELIEVE IT!
The ropes used to wind up siege catapults were made from plaits of human hair!

▶ Cannons were first used to attack castles and fortified towns and cities in the 1300s. Early cannons, called bombards, were made of bronze or iron and they were not very accurate.

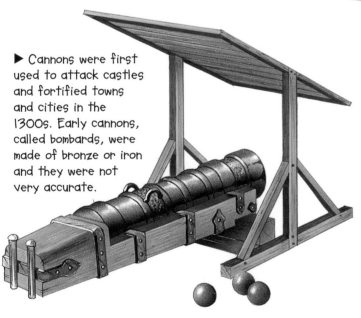

272 The invention of cannons and gunpowder brought the building of castle strongholds almost to an end. It marked the end of warrior knights too. Castle walls could not stand up to the powerful cannonballs that exploded against them. Guns and cannons were now used on the battlefield, so armies no longer needed the services of brave armoured knights on horseback.

Defending a castle

273 When the enemy was first spotted approaching a castle, its defenders first pulled up the castle drawbridge. They also lowered an iron grate, called a portcullis, to form an extra barrier behind the drawbridge.

274 The castle archers fired their arrows through narrow slits in the thick castle walls. They also fired through the gaps in the battlements.

◀ Crossbows were far slower to aim and fire than longbows.

▶ Soldiers could use a longbow while the enemy was still a long way away.

275 In the middle of the night, a raiding party might leave a besieged castle to surprise the enemy camped outside. The raiders would move along secret passages and climb out through hidden gates or doorways.

276 Defenders poured boiling-hot water onto the heads of the enemy as they tried to climb the castle walls. Quicklime was also poured over the enemy soldiers, making their skin burn.

▶ Water was poured onto the enemy's heads through holes in the stonework of the battlements.

277 Heavy stones and other missiles often rained down from the battlements onto the enemy below. Hidden from view by the high battlements, the defenders stood on wooden platforms to throw the missiles.

Quiz

1. What is the name of the mock battles held between large numbers of knights?

2. Which weapon did jousting knights use when on horseback?

3. Which two countries fought a war that lasted 100 years?

4. In what year was the battle of Agincourt?

5. Which machine was used to break down castle walls and gates?

1. tourneys 2. a lance 3. England and France 4. 1415 5. a battering ram

Off to the crusades

278 The crusades were military expeditions from Europe to Palestine. The aim for European Christians was to recapture Palestine, at the eastern end of the Mediterranean Sea, from the Muslim Turks who had seized control of it. The First Crusade set off from Europe in 1096. Between 1096 and 1204 there were four separate crusades.

279 The crusaders built huge castles to defend their lands against the much larger Muslim armies. Many of these castles were big enough to house thousands of soldiers as well as their servants and horses. In the port of Acre the crusaders had constructed a vast underground fortress.

280

Thousands of young boys and girls set off for the Holy Land in 1212 in one of the strangest crusades – the Children's Crusade. Many died of cold or hunger while marching to the Mediterranean ports. Others drowned during the sea crossing, and some were sold as slaves along the way.

281

The Muslim leader Saladin fought against the knights of the Third Crusade. Saladin had already defeated the Christian armies and seized the city of Jerusalem. The Third Crusade was meant to recapture Jerusalem. It was led by an emperor and two kings: Emperor Frederick I of Germany, and Richard the Lionheart of England and Philip II of France, but the crusaders failed to regain Jerusalem.

I DON'T BELIEVE IT!

A crusader knight would share his tent with his beloved horse – it must have been a bit of a squeeze!

282

Many crusaders fought in these religious wars for personal riches. They came from all over western Europe. This was a time when European countries were trying to become more powerful – and wealthier too. Merchants from Italy wanted to increase their trade, knights from France wanted to grow richer, priests from England wanted to collect religious treasures.

Garters and elephants

283 A group of Christian knights living in the Holy Land were in charge of protecting pilgrims on their way to and from Palestine. They were the Templar knights, or Templars. Their headquarters were in the Aqsa Mosque in the city of Jerusalem. The Templars grew very rich during their time in the Holy Land, but their organization was eventually broken up.

284 The Knights of St John looked after the safety and health of pilgrims while they were in the Holy Land. The knights lived like monks and followed strict rules, but they also continued to provide soldiers to fight the Muslims.

▶ The Knights of St John had been monks who cared for sick people before becoming religious knights. They were often referred to as the Hospitallers.

285 Medieval knights began to band together to form special groups called orders. Each order had its own badge showing the symbol chosen by the order. It was considered an honour to be asked to join an order. New orders began to appear in many countries across Europe. The Order of the Golden Fleece, for example, was started in France by Philip the Good.

▲ Knights wore the badge of their order on a chain around the neck. Knights from the Order of the Golden Fleece wore a badge depicting a golden sheep.

286 The Order of the Bath was founded in Britain in the early 1400s. Knights who belonged to an order swore loyalty to their king or queen, and promised to fight against their enemies.

287 The Order of the Garter is the oldest and most important order in Britain. According to the story, Edward III was dancing with a countess when she lost her garter. As the king gave it back to her, he heard the people near him laughing and joking about what they had seen. Angry, the king said that anyone who had evil thoughts should be ashamed. This is still the motto of the order.

▼ The emblem of the Order of the Garter is a dark-blue garter trimmed with gold. Knights of the order wear it on their left leg at important ceremonies.

288 The Order of the Elephant from Denmark is more than 500 years old. Members of the order wear a badge that features a elephant waving its trunk in the air.

Warriors from the East

289 Warrior knights in Japan in the Middle Ages were known as samurai. People in Japan were also divided into different feudal groups, where people in each group served someone in a higher-ranking group. The samurai, like European knights, served a lord. They usually fought on horseback but later on they began to fight more on foot.

▼ The Seljuk Turks were named after their first leader, Seljuk.

290 A long curving sword was a samurai warrior's most treasured possession. Samurai warriors wore armour on the bodies, arms and legs, a helmet and often a crest made up of a pair of horns.

291 The fierce Seljuk Turks fought against Christian knights during the crusades. The Seljuks swept across southwest Asia in the 1000s and 1100s. They conquered many lands, including Syria, Palestine, Asia Minor (modern Turkey) and Persia (modern Iran).

292

Fierce Mongol warriors from the East terrifed the enemy in battle. The Mongols were expert horsemen who controlled their horses with their feet while standing up in their stirrups. This way of riding left both hands free to shoot a bow and arrow.

▼ Each Mongol warrior had a team of five horses ready for battle. As well as being skilled archers, the Mongols were highly trained spear-throwers.

293

Genghis Khan was the greatest of the Mongol leaders. He became leader of his tribe when he was just 13 years old. He united all the Mongol tribes, and went on to conquer northern China, Korea, northern India, Afghanistan, Persia and parts of Russia.

I DON'T BELIEVE IT!

The Turks fought with gold pieces in their mouth – to stop the crusader knights from stealing their gold. If a Turkish warrior thought he was going to die, he swallowed the gold.

Famous castles

294 Many castles are said to be haunted by the ghosts of people who died within their walls. Many of these ghosts are kings and queens who were killed by their sworn enemies. Edward II of England was murdered in his cell at Berkeley Castle in southwest England. Richard II died at Pontefract Castle in Yorkshire.

▲ Visitors to Berkeley Castle say they can hear the screams of the murdered Edward at night.

▲ Windsor Castle

296 Glamis Castle in Scotland is the scene for the play 'Macbeth' by William Shakespeare. In the play, Macbeth plots with his evil wife to kill the Scottish king, Duncan, and claim the throne for himself. In real life, Macbeth did defeat and kill Duncan in 1040.

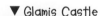

▼ Glamis Castle

▲ Bodiam Castle

295 English kings and queens have lived at Windsor Castle since William the Conqueror began building it more than 900 years ago. William's original castle consisted of a wooden fort on top of an earth motte, with earthworks around the bailey area. The first stone buildings were added in the 1100s.

297 The moated Bodiam Castle in southern England was built in the 1300s to keep out attacking French armies. An English knight, Sir Edward Dalyngrigge, believed that the French were about to invade his lands. His castle home had a curtain wall broken up by round towers.

▼ The castle at Krak des Chevaliers that visitors see today is almost unchanged from the 1300s and 1400s. This remarkable castle was the home of the Hospitaller knights.

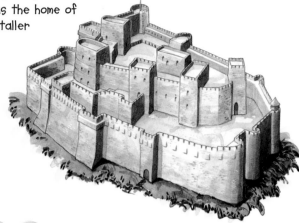

298 The huge crusader castle of Krak des Chevaliers in Syria is perched on a hill of solid rock with far-reaching views over the surrounding countryside. A ditch between the castle's massive outside wall, with its 13 towers, and the inside wall was filled with water from a nearby aqueduct. This moat was used to supply the castle baths and to water the knights' horses.

299 The town of Carcassonne in southern France is rather like one huge castle. The whole town is surrounded by high walls and towers that were built in the Middle Ages.

300 The hilltop castle of Neuschwanstein was built long after the Middle Ages – work on the castle started in 1869. The fairytale castle was the dream project of 'mad' King Ludwig of Bavaria. The government of Bavaria removed the king from power because his ambitious castle-building plans cost too much money.

◀ Today, Neuschwanstein Castle is one of Germany's most popular tourist attractions. The castle was the model for the Magic Kingdom castle in Walt Disney's theme park in California, USA.

The world of pirates

301 **A pirate is a robber on the sea.** Pirates attack ships and ports, stealing treasure and other goods. As soon as the first ships began to carry cargo, pirates began to plunder them – and they are still a threat today. About 500 years ago some areas became special pirate strongholds. The 'corsairs' swooped on vessels in the Mediterranean. The 'buccaneers' of the Caribbean attacked treasure galleons on their way to Europe. The Indian Ocean and the South China Seas were also dangerous places for merchant ships to sail.

Terror from the sea

302 The Greek islands were home to some of the earliest known of all pirates. In around 500BC, there were many cargo ships trading along the Mediterranean coasts. They were easy prey for the pirates, who stole their loads of silver, copper and amber (a precious fossilized resin) before disappearing to their hideouts among the islands.

303 In 67BC, the Roman leader Pompey sent a huge fleet to wipe out the pirates of the Mediterranean. They had become a threat to the city of Rome itself by stealing grain supplies. For several years, the Roman campaign got rid of the pirate menace.

304
Pirates in ancient times used small, fast ships with shallow bottoms. They could steer them easily, and escape into small bays and channels where bigger boats could not follow.

305
Julius Caesar was captured by pirates when he was 25. While a prisoner, he joked that he would come back and kill them all. In the end, he was released – and kept his promise. Caesar's troops seized and executed the pirates a few months later.

306
Viking ships crossed the North Sea to raid settlements on the British coast. Bands of up to 50 Vikings terrified Britons with their battle axes and wide two-edged swords. Their speedy flat-bottomed 'longships' could even carry them up rivers to attack villages inland.

PICTURE PUZZLE

This Greek ship called a trireme was used to fight pirates. It had three banks of rowers on each side. Count them up and see how many were needed to push the trireme along.

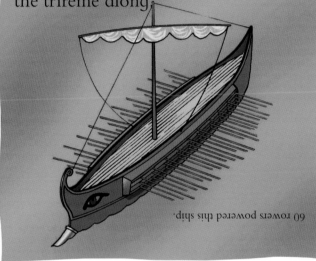

60 rowers powered this ship.

Muslim marauders

307 **Pirates of the Mediterranean were known as 'corsairs'.** The most famous corsairs were Muslims from the Barbary Coast of North Africa. They took great delight in plundering Christian ships – especially when the two sides were at war after the crusades began in about 1100.

308 **The corsairs wanted people, not treasure.** They sold their ordinary captives as slaves, or forced them to work in their galleys. Richer people were more valuable. The corsairs demanded ransoms for their release.

This is a pirate blunderbuss. The wider end, or muzzle, was designed to spread the shot widely before before boarding a ship.

cannon ball

early grenade

dagger

dagger sheath

309
At the front of the ship a corsair galley had a massive ram. The galley was rammed into the side of the Christian vessel. Then soldiers called janissaries jumped aboard and quickly captured the enemy.

310
Corsairs fought with curved swords called scimitars. Muslim craftsmen made the sharpest and most beautiful swords and daggers in the world. Some corsairs also carried muskets, while the galleys were armed with small brass cannon.

311
The two most feared corsairs were the Barbarossa brothers. One attacked ships belonging to the Pope and even captured the town of Algiers in north Africa, but he was killed there in 1518. The other Barbarossa became an ally of the Turkish emperor.

I DON'T BELIEVE IT!

'Barbarossa' was not the brothers' real name. It was a nickname given to them by their enemies because of the colour of their beards. Barba rossa means 'Redbeard' in Latin.

Captured by corsairs

312 **The life of a galley slave was horrible.** The oars were so big and heavy that they needed as many as six men to pull them. The slaves were chained to rows of benches. In between the rows strode the overseer, or officer in charge. He would drive the men to work harder, either by shouting or by lashing them with his whip.

313 **On land, the slaves lived in a prison, or bagnio.** Each slave had a heavy ring and chain riveted to his ankle, and was given a blanket to sleep on. When he was not rowing in the galleys, he spent his time digging or breaking rocks. There was little food apart from bread, and many slaves died in the bagnio.

▼ Going to sea in a stolen, or even a hand-made boat, was the only way for slaves to escape.

314 **Many slaves tried to escape.** Some went inland, but found only desert regions short of food and water. The only other way was to escape by sea, making or stealing a boat. Very few got away.

315 **There were Christian corsairs too.** Many were based on the island of Malta, where they were supported by Christian knights on the island who wanted to see the Muslims defeated. Maltese corsairs also used galleys rowed by men captured and forced to work, and were just as brutal as their enemies in North Africa.

▼ The English and Dutch fleet bombarded Algiers with cannon to stop the corsairs and free their slaves.

316 **In 1816 English and Dutch ships bombarded Algiers.** They forced the corsairs to release over 3,000 slaves. A few years later French troops invaded Algiers, and brought the ravages of the corsair bands to an end.

317 **Some corsairs attacked countries far from the Mediterranean.** Murad Rais sailed all the way to Iceland in 1627. His plundered treasure included salted fish and leather!

The Spanish Main

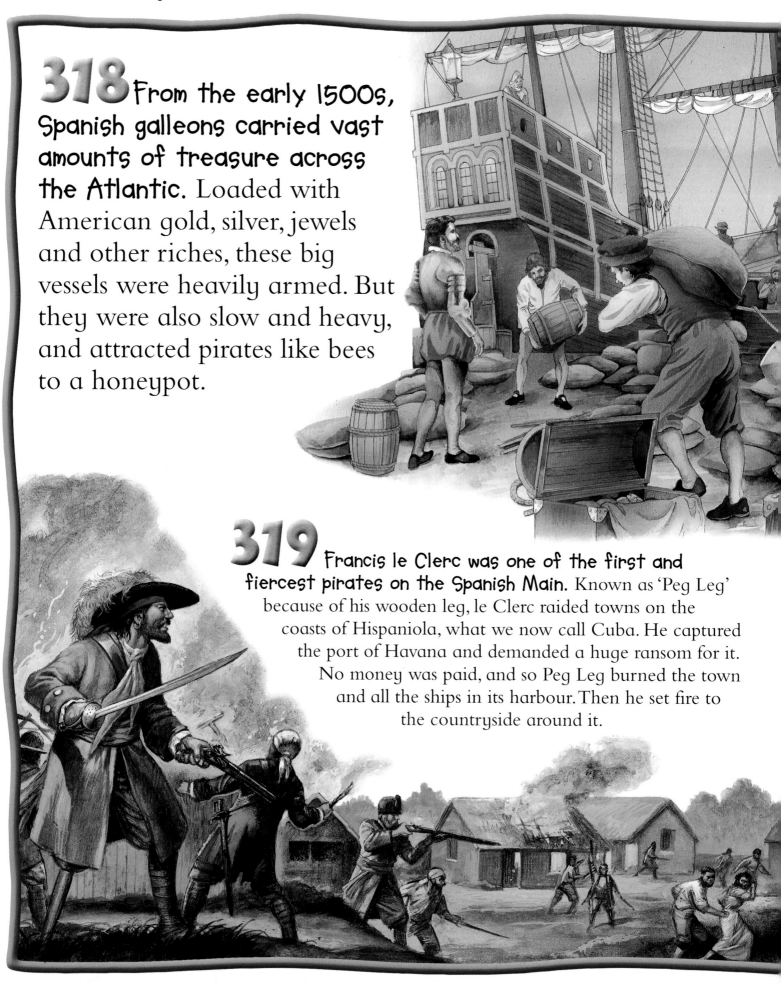

318 From the early 1500s, Spanish galleons carried vast amounts of treasure across the Atlantic. Loaded with American gold, silver, jewels and other riches, these big vessels were heavily armed. But they were also slow and heavy, and attracted pirates like bees to a honeypot.

319 Francis le Clerc was one of the first and fiercest pirates on the Spanish Main. Known as 'Peg Leg' because of his wooden leg, le Clerc raided towns on the coasts of Hispaniola, what we now call Cuba. He captured the port of Havana and demanded a huge ransom for it. No money was paid, and so Peg Leg burned the town and all the ships in its harbour. Then he set fire to the countryside around it.

▼ The soldiers guarding the treasure were called 'conquistadores', who were the first of the Spanish soldiers to invade South America. They often travelled with the treasure ships, but were no match for the pirates.

PICTURE PUZZLE

Can you spot the different kinds of treasure hidden aboard this galleon?

You should be able to spot gold, jewels and 'pieces of eight'.

320 Soon the Spaniards began to assemble their galleons into fleets. They realised that groups of ships would be safer from pirates than single ones. Two big fleets arrived in the Spanish Main each year. One loaded up with treasure from Mexico. The other went to Panama, where it took on silver brought overland from mines in Peru, and treasures ferried across the Pacific from the Philippines. Small and heavily armed warships protected the treasure fleets as they made their way back home to Spain.

treasure ships

armed warships

▲ The treasure ships, the large ships in the middle, always sailed across the Atlantic with heavily armed warships on either side of them.

Sea dogs

321 John Hawkins made many raids on Spanish treasure ships. But he did not call himself a pirate. He carried a letter from his Queen, Elizabeth I of England, which allowed him to attack ships from an enemy nation. England and Spain were not at war, but they were enemies. Hawkins, and many like him, were called 'privateers'.

▲ This letter of marque was issued by King George III of England. Genuine letters contained restrictions on which ships they could attack.

322 Hawkins' voyages made him very rich. He sailed first to West Africa where he rounded up 400 slaves and loaded them on board. Next he sailed to the Caribbean where he sold the slaves in exchange for gold, silver and pearls.

323 Walter Raleigh never found any gold in South America. He made two voyages in search of the fabulous gold-encrusted man – El Dorado. Both voyages were failures, and when he returned, Raleigh was beheaded.

▲ The slave trade lasted for hundreds of years. Up to 70,000 slaves were transported in horrible conditions every year. Some people say that a total of 15 million slaves were delivered, but many millions died on the way.

324

Francis Drake was the greatest of the Elizabethan 'sea dogs'. He first went to sea at 14, and later joined his cousin John Hawkins on his expeditions. Like Hawkins, he became a privateer, and carried on an unofficial war against Spain.

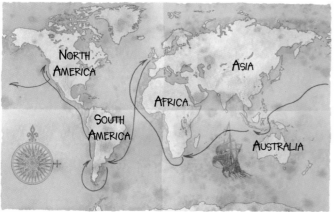

▲ The route of Drake's three-year voyage round the world.

326
In 1572 Drake attacked Spanish settlements in Panama.

He ambushed a mule train laden with silver at Nombre de Dios. He became the first Englishman to see the Pacific Ocean. He vowed that one day he would sail there.

325
Drake's most amazing exploit was his voyage round the world.

He set out in 1577 and found his way to the Pacific. Here he captured the giant Spanish treasure ship 'Cacafuego', which was carrying a cargo worth over £12 million in today's money. By the time Drake got back to England in 1580, his two remaining ships were crammed with riches as well.

I DON'T BELIEVE IT!
When Drake raided the treasure store at Nombre de Dios, he landed at night, captured the guns and fought off the guards. But when the store was opened, it was empty!

Pig hunters

327 The original buccaneers were drifters and criminals on the island of Hispaniola, modern Cuba. They wandered about, hunting the wild pigs for food. They cooked them over wood fires.

328 During the 1630s, the Spanish drove out these 'buccaneers' and killed all the wild pigs. So the buccaneer bands, who had to find food somewhere, became pirates instead. They began to attack and loot passing Spanish merchant ships.

329 The first buccaneer stronghold was a small rocky island called Tortuga. It had a sheltered harbour, and was close to the main shipping route. Buccaneers built a fort at Tortuga and placed 24 cannons there, pointing out to sea.

330 Henry Morgan started out as a privateer, but soon became a famous buccaneer leader. In 1668 he led an army overland to sack the city of Portobello in Cuba. Two years later, Morgan conquered Panama City, and opened the way for pirates into the Pacific.

There are six pirate weapons hidden in this picture. Can you find a scimitar, a dagger, a pistol, a musket, an axe and a firebomb?

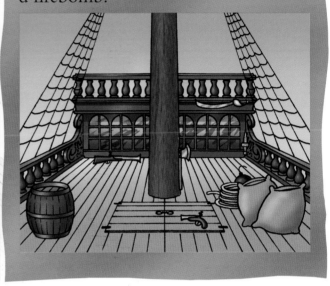

331
The name of Francis L'Ollonais struck terror into Spanish hearts. This buccaneer became famous for his cruel and heartless deeds. This meant that people were more likely to surrender straight away when they knew it was him.

332
The buccaneers even invented a special kind of sword – the cutlass. This began as a knife which they used for cutting up the wild pigs. It soon became a broad, short sword which many pirates and other sailors carried as their main weapon in battle.

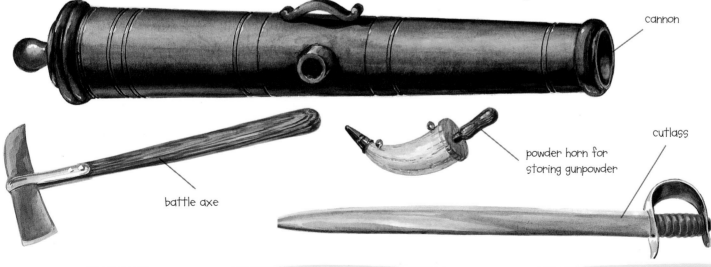

cannon

battle axe

powder horn for storing gunpowder

cutlass

Pirate stronghold

333 In the 1650s, most buccaneers moved to a new hideout on Jamaica. This was Port Royal, set at the end of a narrow spit of land. There was a fort to guard the harbour entrance, and docks where pirates could repair their ships. The British, who ruled Jamaica, did not try to interfere with the buccaneers. Port Royal was a pirate paradise!

334 Port Royal was a wild and wealthy place. The buccaneers brought their plunder to the docks to sell to merchants. With the money they roamed the streets looking for a good time. The town had 44 taverns, crowded with drunkards, pickpockets and runaway slaves as well as pirates. The money disappeared fast. One citizen wrote that the buccaneers "have been known to spend 3,000 pieces of eight [silver coins] in one night". That is £45,000 in today's money.

335 Port Royal was destroyed by a monster earthquake in 1692. Buildings collapsed, and two whole streets were swallowed up by the sea. A giant wave followed the earthquake, washing right over the town. Altogether, 4,000 people died in the disaster. Some saw it as God's punishment for their wicked ways.

QUIZ 2

1. What kind of meat did the first buccaneers eat?

2. Which island did they live on?

3. What kind of sword did the buccaneers invent?

4. Where were the treasure galleons going?

5. What were pieces of eight?

1. wild pig 2. Hispaniola 3. the cutlass 4. Spain 5. silver coins

Island of thieves

336 Pirates had prowled the Indian Ocean for many centuries. From bases on the Indian coast, over 100 pirate ships put to sea. They scoured the ocean all summer, seizing the cargoes of lone merchant ships.

337 When Portuguese sailors reached the Indian Ocean, they soon became pirates too. From about 1500, Portuguese traders began sailing from Africa to India, and then on to the Far East. They stole silks, spices, jewels and gold from the Arab merchants.

338 The exotic treasures of the East quickly attracted many buccaneers. They moved from the Caribbean to the Indian Ocean, many settling on the island of Madagascar. This was a wild and unexplored land, where it was easy to hide.

▲ The large island of Madagascar lies at the southeast corner of Africa. Its remote and forested coast made a perfect stronghold for pirates.

339 William Kidd started out as a pirate-hunter, but became a pirate! He was sent to chase pirates in the Indian Ocean in 1696. Within a few months, Kidd was attacking ordinary trading ships, including the 'Queddah Merchant' whose cargo he sold for £10,000. When he returned home he was arrested and hanged for piracy. His body was displayed in a cage at the mouth of the Thames for several years.

340
Henry Avery was feared as 'The Arch Pirate'. His most ferocious deed was the capture of the Indian Emperor's treasure ship in the Red Sea. He tortured many passengers, and terrified the women so much that they jumped overboard.

341
Kanhoji Angria was the greatest of the Indian Ocean pirates. Setting sail from India's west coast, he led his ships against any merchant ships which passed. He also built a series of forts along the coast, and defied the strength of the British navy. His followers were called 'Angrians'.

PIRATE SEARCH

The surnames of seven pirates and privateers are hidden in this letter square. Can you find them all?

```
B R N A D C X M
D R A K E B N O
L E C L E R C R
K R K S E S W G
L O I A A I G A
D S D N L S G N
C Y D T E A C H
```

Drake, Raleigh, Morgan, Le Clerc, Read, Kidd, Teach

151

Junks and outriggers

342 **The South China Seas were a perfect place for pirates.** There was a maze of small islands, mangrove swamps and narrow channels to hide in, and many merchant ships to ambush. Chinese pirates became famous for their violence and brutal methods.

344 Ching-Chi-Ling was the first great Chinese pirate leader. With his fleet of more than 1,000 junks, he brought terror to the coast of China.

343 **Chinese pirates sailed in ships called junks.** These were often captured trading vessels, with three masts carrying square bamboo sails. The pirate captain lived in the stern cabin with his family, while his men often slept on the open deck. Junks were armed with cannon, while sailors had muskets and pistols.

▶ The Chinese had been sailing their junks for hundreds of years. A general called Zheng-he commanded ocean-going junks in the 1200s that were five times larger than European ships of the time.

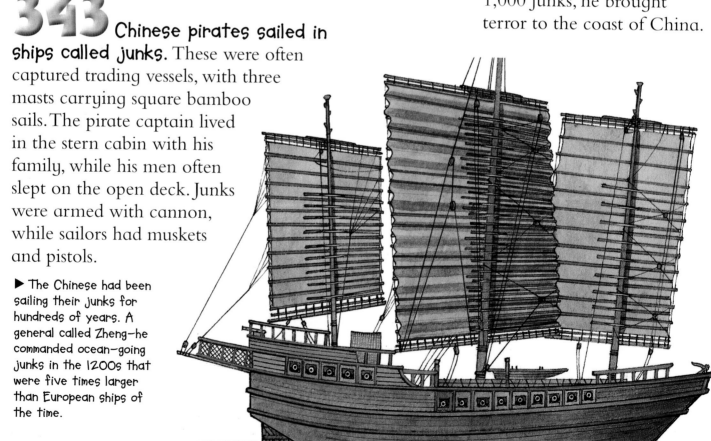

▲ With their huge fleets of pirate junks, Chinese pirates like Ching–Chi–Ling and Shap–'ng–tsai wielded huge power in the South China Sea and through to the Indian Ocean.

QUIZ 3

1. Which of these is not a type of ship?
   Galleon, junk, rowlock, galley, outrigger
2. Which of these is not a type of pirate weapon?
   Musket, ball valve, cutlass, sumpitan, parang
3. Where did the Balanini pirates come from?

1. rowlock 2. ball valve 3. the islands of Sulu

345 The Balanini pirates came from the islands of Sulu. They sailed in small, speedy canoes with extra beams called outriggers. In these, the Balanini swooped down on the nearby islands, kidnapping hundreds of slaves to sell in the mainland markets.

346 British ships were sent to wipe out the last great pirate fleet in 1849. They chased the junks, led by Shap–'ng–tsai, for over 1,000 miles before they caught them. Then they blew the junks to pieces and killed over 1,800 pirates. Shap–'ng–tsai escaped and lived to a ripe old age, but the pirate menace was ended – for the time being.

347 South Seas pirates used a great many fearsome weapons. They shot poisoned arrows through a blowpipe called a sumpitan. They brandished a razor-sharp chopping sword called a parang, or a knife called a kris. Some knives were completely straight, others had a rippled effect. Some were straight near the handle, or hilt, but were curved at the end. Some weapons were decorated with human hair.

◄ A kris, or 'flashing blade', used by pirates from Borneo, with its wooden scabbard.

Women pirates

348 Mary Read dressed in man's clothes so that she could become a sailor. But her ship was captured by pirates on its way to the West Indies, and Mary was taken prisoner. She joined the pirates, and then became a privateer. Once again, her ship fell victim to rival sea robbers, this time to 'Calico Jack' Rackham and his wife Anne Bonny. The two women were soon close friends. In a battle against the British navy, they both fought like demons while the rest of the crew (all men) hid below!

▶ When Grace O'Malley was pardoned for her piracy, she didn't exactly give up altogether. She just handed her business over to her sons who carried it on!

349 Grace O'Malley commanded a pirate fleet on Ireland's west coast. She went to sea as a young girl, and later moved into a massive stone castle right on the coast. Her fleet of twenty sailing ships and rowing boats attacked passing merchant vessels. In 1593 Grace gave up her piratical ways and begged Queen Elizabeth for a pardon. She lived to be over 70 years old.

I DON'T BELIEVE IT!

While she was a pirate Grace O'Malley cut her hair short to look like her sailors. This earned her the nickname of 'Baldy'!

350 One of the greatest woman pirates was Ching Shih. When her husband died in 1807, she took over his raiding fleet on the Chinese coast. She was a brilliant leader, and forced her sailors to obey a strict set of rules. But life on her pirate junks was not pleasant. One captive recalled "we lived three weeks on caterpillars boiled in rice".

All aboard!

351 Most pirate ships had to be small and fast. On the Spanish Main, many were 'schooners', with two masts, and many were galleys with three masts like this one. The captain's cabin was in the stern, while the crew slept in the middle of the ship. Treasure, gunpowder and food stores were kept in the hold.

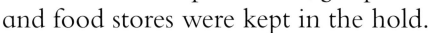

mizzen topsail main topsail mainsail fore topsail foresail

stern (back)

sail locker

water and stores

oars

bow (front)

bowsprit

352 Below decks, it was very cramped and smelly. There was little space for the crew to sleep. Pirates barely had room to put up their hammocks, and spent most of their lives on deck, except in the worst weather.

353 Food was mostly horrid on board a pirate ship. The cook was often a pirate who had lost an arm and couldn't do anything else. And he seldom had anything to serve except dry biscuits and pickled meat. Whenever the crew landed on a remote island, they hunted for fresh meat and – even more important – fresh water.

354
In calm weather, there was little for the pirates to do. They would mend ropes and sails, or gamble with dice. In bad weather, or when they were chasing another ship, life was very busy. The crew might have to climb aloft in the rigging to alter the sails, keep lookout from high on the mainmast, or prepare the cannon for firing.

355
The hull of the ship had to be kept clean. Weeds and barnacles would slow it down, so pirates regularly dragged their vessel up onto a beach where they could scrape off any rubbish. This was also a chance to go hunting for food.

DRESS UP AS A PIRATE

Tie a red scarf round your head. Put on trousers, shirt and waistcoat – as brightly coloured as you can find. Earrings are easy, and it's not hard to make your own black moustache (out of wool) and eyepatch (cardboard and elastic bands). Now all you need is a bloodcurdling pirate yell!

356
Most pirates dressed just like other sailors of the time. They wore short blue jackets, checked shirts and baggy canvas trousers. But some showed off the finery they had stolen, such as velvet trousers, black felt hats, silk shirts and crimson waistcoats with gold buttons and gold lace.

▶ If a pirate had stolen clothing, they would often just sell it. But if they liked something, they may just wear it!

Attack!

357

When a captain decided to attack, he raised a 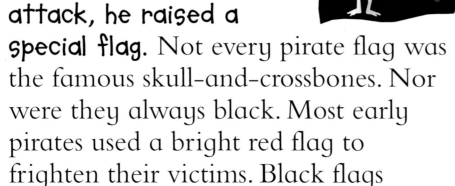 special flag. Not every pirate flag was the famous skull-and-crossbones. Nor were they always black. Most early pirates used a bright red flag to frighten their victims. Black flags  became popular in the early 1700s, with pirates adding their own initials or symbols.

358 Pirates depended on speed to catch their prey. If they had cannon, they would try and hit the other ship's mast or rigging. Otherwise, they fired muskets at the helmsman and other men working in the sails. In this way they could slow the ship down. If they got near enough, they might even jam the rudder so that it would not steer properly.

359 A pirate bristled with weapons. His cutlass was in his hand, and a dagger was in his belt. He might carry as many as six loaded pistols tied to a sash which he wore over his shoulder.

360 When they were near enough the attackers threw ropes with hooked grappling irons into the rigging. The ship was caught – just like a fish. The pirates climbed up the sides and jumped aboard. Sometimes they had a bloody fight on their hands. But often the enemy crew were so terrified that they surrendered straight away.

DESIGN A PIRATE FLAG

You can have your very own personal pirate flag. On a black background, draw your own scary design using bones, skulls and anything else you fancy. No-one else is allowed to copy it!

361 Merchants often hid their cargo. The pirates had to search everywhere and tear apart walls and doors to find it. They might even torture their captives until they told them where the treasure was.

362

Bartholomew Roberts was probably the most successful pirate ever. Known as Black Bart, he captured as many as 400 ships in the 1720s. Handsome, bold, he was everyone's ideal buccaneer. Yet he never drank anything stronger than tea!

◀ One of the best ways to slow a ship was to fire at the sails and rigging.

Pirate plunder

363 **All pirates dreamed of gold and silver.** Some were lucky enough to capture ships packed with them – in the form of coins, gold bars or finely made ornaments. But most merchant ships carried humbler goods, such as cloth, coal or iron.

▲ After capturing a cargo vessel, the pirates transfer all the treasure and other valuables to their own ship.

364 **The most famous coins of the Spanish Main were 'pieces of eight' or simply pesos.** These were silver, and as big as a 50 pence piece. Each one was worth about £15 in today's money.

365 **Silk and porcelain were the most precious goods from China.** For centuries, no-one in Europe knew how silk or porcelain (fine earthenware) were made. They were very delicate, and pirates had to handle them carefully.

366 People could be valuable

as well. Pirates might hold a rich captive and demand a ransom from their relatives. When this was paid, the prisoner was freed.

367 Some treasure chests

were full of jewels. There were diamonds from Africa, rubies and sapphires from Burma and pearls from the Persian Gulf. Many of these were made up into beautiful jewellery.

I DON'T BELIEVE IT!

One of the most valuable cargoes of all were the spices from India and Sri Lanka. But they were difficult to sell, and pirates simply dumped them overboard. One beach was said to be ankle deep in precious spices.

368 Pirates also needed

everyday things. If they had been away from land for several weeks, they would be glad to steal food, drink and other provisions. And fresh guns, cannon balls and gunpowder always came in useful!

▲ Pirates wait eagerly as their captain shares out the treasure.

369 The captain shared out

the loot among his crew. He did this very carefully, so that no-one could complain. All the same, officers got more than the men, and the carpenter and cook got less – because they didn't fight.

Buried treasure

370 **Pirates often hid their treasure by burying it in a remote spot.** Then they could come back and dig it up when times were quieter. After his attack on a mule train in Panama, Francis Drake found that his ship had sailed out of sight. He ordered his men to bury the looted gold and silver. Then he made a raft, paddled out to find his ships, and brought them back. That night, his men dug up the treasure and put it on board.

371
Many believe that William Kidd buried a vast store of treasure before he was captured. His piracy had gained him a huge amount of cargo, most of which he sold off or gave to his crew. But when he was arrested in 1699 he claimed that he had hidden £100,000 of treasure. Since then, hundreds of people have looked for it all over the world – but none has found a single coin.

▶ Pirates lived in a rough and dangerous world. There was no code of conduct between ships, so there was no reason for a pirate ship not to steal the treasure from another pirate ship!

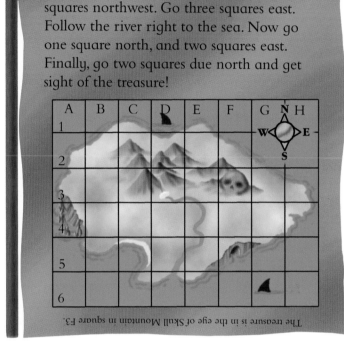

BURIED TREASURE

Can you follow the trail and find the buried treasure?

Start on a crescent shape of sand. Go two squares northwest. Go three squares east. Follow the river right to the sea. Now go one square north, and two squares east. Finally, go two squares due north and get sight of the treasure!

The treasure is in the eye of Skull Mountain in square F3.

372
The pirates of the ship 'Mary Dear' buried their loot in the Cocos Islands of the Pacific in 1820. It included over 12,000 gemstones and 9,000 gold coins, as well as seven chests of gold ornaments. Then the pirates set the ship on fire and rowed off in the longboats. When they reached land, they were arrested. None of the pirates ever went back to dig up the treasure, and no-one has discovered it since!

Desert islands

373 Some pirate captains had strict rules. 'Black Bart' Roberts made his crew promise to keep to a code of conduct. They must not gamble or fight on board ship, or keep lights and candles burning after 8 o'clock at night. Anyone who brought a woman on board, or who deserted the ship, would be put to death or marooned.

374 Marooning was a terrible fate. The pirate was left alone on a deserted island while his friends sailed away. He was given a pistol and ammunition, and a bottle of water. But it was almost impossible to escape, and food was hard to find. The only hope was to be picked up by another ship.

Goat Rock

Selkirk's island was called Más á Tierra.

NORTH AMERICA

ASIA

AFRICA

SOUTH AMERICA

• Más á Tierra

Goat Quarters

Open Bay

Sharpes Bay

Sugar Loaf Key

Windy Bay

377 The most famous of all castaways was Alexander Selkirk.
He was stranded on a desert island off the coast of Chile in 1704, and stayed there for five years. Selkirk was very lucky, for his island had plenty of fresh water, along with wild pigs and goats. At last, dressed in goat skins, he was rescued by a passing English ship. Writer Daniel Defoe based his story of 'Robinson Crusoe' on Selkirk's adventures.

◄ The group of islands on which Selkirk was marooned were the Juan Fernandez islands. He was very lucky that he had plenty of food and water.

375 The Pacific and the Caribbean were dotted with thousands of small islands. Very few had people living on them. Many were far away from the main shipping routes. The castaway had to hunt for fruit and small animals, or fish in the warm seas.

376 Sometimes the crew marooned their captain. This happened to Jeremy Rendell in 1684. After an argument with his crew, he was left on an island near Honduras with three other men, a gun, a canoe and a net for catching turtles. They were never heard from again.

PICTURE PUZZLE

You've been marooned on a desert island. Somewhere are hidden a water bottle, a pistol, a knife, a blanket, a kettle and an axe. Can you find them?

Storm and shipwreck

378 **Shipwreck was a pirate's biggest nightmare.** Violent storms could spring up suddenly, especially in the warm seas of the Caribbean. In 1712, a hurricane brought racing winds and giant waves into Port Royal harbour in Jamaica, smashing 38 ships.

379 **Storms could drive helpless ships onto a rocky shore.** In 1717 the pirate ship 'Whydah' was heading for Cape Cod, off North America, loaded with booty. A storm sprang up, pushing the vessel onto rocks. The mainmast fell down, and the 'Whydah' started to break up. Only two of the crew reached land alive.

381 **A hole in the hull had to be patched – fast!** The quickest way was to 'fother' it, by lowering a sail with ropes so that it fitted over the hole. But sails were not very watertight, and the patch did not last long.

380 **There were few ways to cope with an emergency.** If the ship was leaking, sailors could try pumping out the water. If the ship ran aground, they could throw heavy objects overboard, such as cannon or food barrels. This made the ship lighter, and ride higher in the water.

QUIZ 4

1. Your ship is stuck on a sandbar. How do you get off?

2. What instrument tells you where north is?

3. What could you use as an emergency patch for a hole?

4. Name two things you might be left with if you were marooned.

1. Throw heavy objects overboard 2. compass 3. a sail 4. you can have a pistol, a water bottle and ammunition

382 Pirates had to find their way across the sea by skill and a lot of luck. Tools for navigating were still very simple. The captain had a compass to show his bearing, or direction, and an octant or sextant which showed how far north or south he was. But his longitude (position east or west) was mostly a matter of guesswork.

383 William Dampier was an expert navigator, who sailed around the world three times. He joined the buccaneers of Jamaica for a short time, before heading off to explore the southern Pacific. He was one of the first Europeans to see Australia.

telescope

compass

backstaff

dividers

map

Hunting the pirates

384 European countries began to build bigger and stronger navies. With these, they were able to begin sweeping the pirates from the seas. Well-armed navy fleets patrolled the trouble spots. Pirates were offered free pardons if they gave up their lives of crime. Large rewards were given to anyone who helped to capture pirate ships.

385 Edward Teach was the most terrifying pirate on the high seas. Better known as 'Blackbeard', he made himself look as frightening as possible. He plaited ribbons into his long beard, carried six pistols slung over his shoulder, and stuck lighted matches under his hat. But one man was not afraid of Blackbeard – naval officer Robert Maynard. In 1718 he cornered the pirate, who shouted "Damnation seize my soul if I give you quarter!" Maynard leapt aboard his ship and fought him to the death. Then he cut off Blackbeard's hairy head and hung it in the bows of his vessel.

PICTURE PUZZLE

Which pirate names do these pictures make you think of?

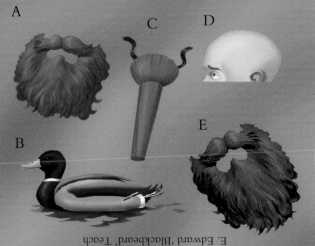

A

C   D

B

E

A. Barbarossa ('red beard') brothers B. Francis Drake C. Francois 'Peg-leg' Le Clerc D. Grace 'Baldy' O'Malley E. Edward 'Blackbeard' Teach

386 Steam power spelled the end for most pirates. The navy built steam ships, which could travel much faster than the old sailing ships and did not depend on the wind. The pirates simply couldn't get away!

On the gallows

387 Many captured pirates were taken back to Britain in chains. But most never got that far. They were taken to the nearest American port and executed as quickly as possible. Only the younger criminals of 15 or 16 years old were pardoned and released.

▲ Captured prisoners were manacled together with long chains on the voyage to prison and trial.

388 Trials in Britain lasted only one or two days. The judges were keen to condemn the pirates as quickly as possible, so that they would frighten those still at large. Anyone who was known to have fired a cannon, carried a gun or taken part in looting was found guilty.

389 Before and after trial, the pirates were kept in prison. In London, this would probably be the hated Newgate Prison, which was foul-smelling, dirty and overcrowded. Many prisoners died of disease or starvation before they ever came to be executed.

▲ Newgate Prison in London was a brutal, unhealthy place.

◀ This is one of the dreaded 'hulks'. These were naval ships that had got too old to be used for sailing, so were converted and used as floating prisons for the worst criminals.

391 The bodies were left on the gallows until the tide came in and covered them.

After three tides, it was either taken down and buried or left hanging in chains as a lesson for others. Some bodies were coated in tar so that they would last longer.

I DON'T BELIEVE IT!

After William Duell was hanged his body was taken down and washed. Then someone saw that he was still breathing! The courts did not have the heart to hang him again, so he was sent to Australia instead.

390 Pirates that had been found guilty were hanged at Execution Dock in London.

They sometimes took a long time to die. William Kidd had to be hanged a second time after the rope broke. As a deterrent, a warning to other people who might become pirates, their bodies were displayed in cages.

▶ An iron cage, used to display the bodies of executed pirates.

392 The British navy destroyed many pirate ships.

An entire fleet of Chinese junks was sunk or set on fire near Hong Kong in 1849, and 400 pirates killed. The naval commander went on to smash up the pirate dockyards and confiscate all the weapons.

Pirates today

393 **Pirates are not a thing of the past.** There are still plenty of pirates operating on the seas today, especially in the Caribbean and the Far East. In 1992, there were more than 90 attacks on ships in just one part of the world – the narrow Straits of Malacca between Singapore and Sumatra. The modern day pirates move in at dead of night in small boats, and climb up ropes or bamboo poles onto the decks of the merchant ships. Within a few minutes they have stolen all the valuables on board, slipped over the side again and disappeared into the dark.

▶ Modern pirates work in a very different way to the pirates from years ago. They prefer to use stealth. This means that they do not climb onto a ship yelling and letting off fireworks as Blackbeard would have done. They prefer to sneak quietly onto a ship take what they want and leave with as little fuss as possible.

394 Modern pirates use modern weapons.

They use machine guns, automatic rifles and speed boats. They plan their attacks with radios and computers.

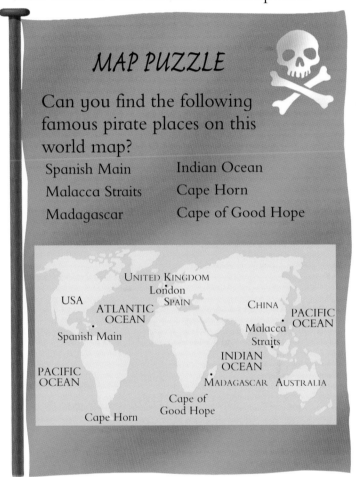

MAP PUZZLE

Can you find the following famous pirate places on this world map?

Spanish Main   Indian Ocean

Malacca Straits   Cape Horn

Madagascar   Cape of Good Hope

UNITED KINGDOM
London
USA   Spain
ATLANTIC
OCEAN   CHINA
                              PACIFIC
                              OCEAN
                    Malacca
Spanish Main   Straits

                    INDIAN
                    OCEAN
PACIFIC
OCEAN   MADAGASCAR AUSTRALIA

          Cape of
          Good Hope
    Cape Horn

395 People are still searching for pirate treasure.

One of the most mysterious sites is Oak Island, off the North American coast. Treasure hunters have been digging here since 1795, when three boys began to dig a pit and found a wooden platform. Was this the place where Captain Kidd or other pirates buried their plunder? Since then, diggers have gone down over 100 metres into the ground, but not a single coin has been found.

Myth and reality

396 The best-known pirate of all is in a story book – Long John Silver. Robert Louis Stevenson's 'Treasure Island' is one of the most exciting and best-loved of all adventure stories. With its one-legged villain (Silver), its crazy castaway (Ben Gunn) and its buried treasure, this has thrilled countless readers since it first appeared in 1883. 'Treasure Island' has also been made into several films.

▲ Robert Louis Stevenson

▲ A scene from Robert Louis Stevenson's 'Treasure Island'. You can see Long John Silver with his parrot, the wild castaway Ben Gunn, and, of course, the treasure!

397 Another famous make-believe pirate is Captain Hook. This nasty character appears in J.M.Barrie's fantasy 'Peter Pan'. One of his hands has been cut off by the hero Peter Pan and fed to a crocodile, so the Captain has a hook instead. The play of 'Peter Pan' is staged every Christmas in London.

398 Many of us get our ideas of pirates from watching films. Ever since cinema began, pirate films have been popular. Great actors have starred in them, from Douglas Fairbanks and Errol Flynn to Dustin Hoffman and Mel Gibson. But these films usually show a very romantic and fun-filled picture of pirate life, and leave out most of the pain and savagery.

399 There are cartoon pirates too.

Many picture books feature jolly pirates who are not frightening at all! The best-known of these is Captain Pugwash, who is not just stupid, but cowardly as well. Only his cabin boy Tom saves him from complete disaster at the hands of his arch-enemy, Cut-throat Jake.

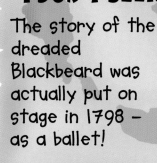

◀ Real pirates were never as kind-hearted as the jolly 'Pirates of Penzance'.

400 The most unlikely pirates of all appear on the stage in an operetta.

'The Pirates of Penzance', created by Gilbert and Sullivan, are real softies who refuse to rob orphans. Needless to say, all their victims claim to be orphans!

Where was the Wild West?

401 North America is a vast continent. When the first Europeans settled on the east coast in the early 1600s they had no idea about the country to the west. During the next 300 years pioneers, early settlers and explorers, moved steadily into the West to fill up the huge empty spaces. They explored, cleared wilderness for farms, dug mines and built towns and railroads. Their lives were often harsh and violent. There were brutal fights over gold and cattle and land, and wars to crush the native peoples. This is why we remember it as the Wild West.

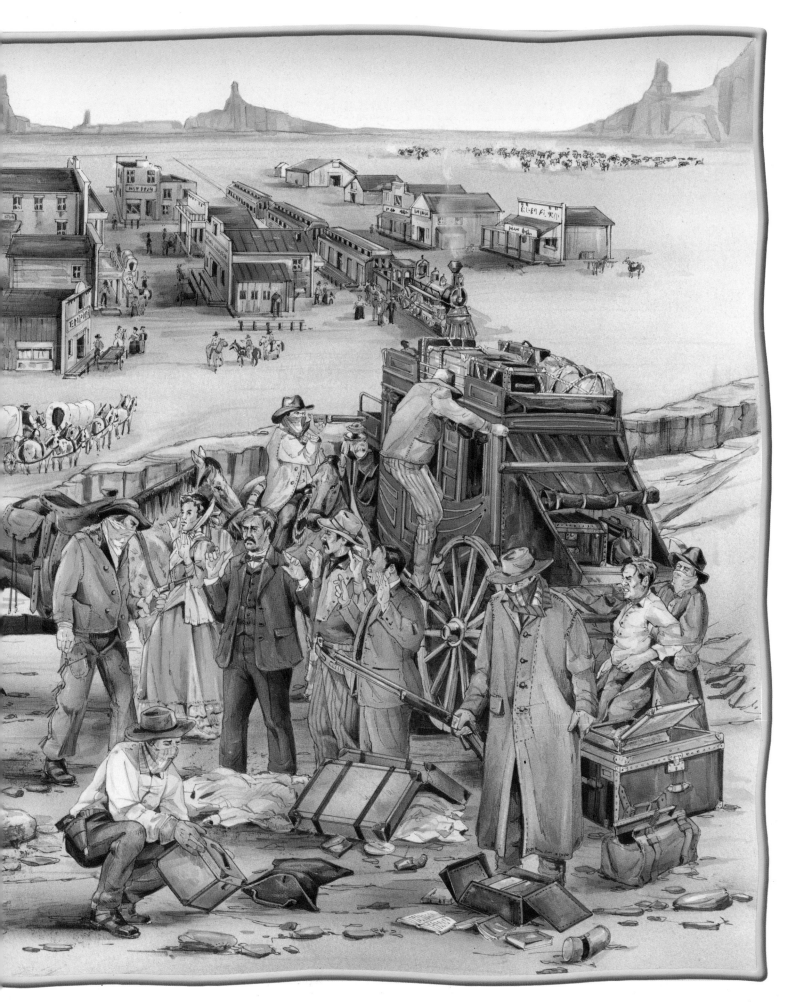

The first Americans

402 The first American people came from Asia. About 20,000 years ago the sea level was lower, leaving a strip of land uncovered between the two continents. People wandered across this, and gradually spread out through America. When Columbus arrived, there were about 20 million Native Americans living here.

▲ The areas in which they lived shaped the ways that the Native American tribes survived. The map shows where the various peoples lived.

403 Tribes of the Northeastern woodlands were never short of food. There were fish and animals to hunt, and crops such as corn and beans grew well. They also made sugar from maple sap.

► The Iroquois people of the Northeast lived in timber long houses and hunted with bows and blowpipes.

404 Before the Europeans arrived, few people lived on the Plains. The soil was hard to dig, and the only fertile land was near rivers. In summer, the Plains tribes hunted herds of buffalo on foot.

◄ Men of the Plains tribes followed the huge herds of buffalo. In autumn they went back home to harvest their crops.

405
Life was simple for Native Americans of California. Tribes such as the Hupa gathered wild foods, such as acorns and seeds, and needed few clothes because the climate was warm. Tribes in these areas rarely went to war with each other.

▲ A summer shelter built by the Hupa people of California on the Pacific Coast.

◀ The Hopi dressed in simple skirts made of leather or woven grasses.

I DON'T BELIEVE IT!
The Flathead people really had flattened heads! Mothers bound boards to their babies' heads to squash them down!

406
The Southwest is a vast dry region of America. Native Americans such as the Hopi, grew crops along the rivers. Corn was so important to them that they worshipped it as a god. The Pueblo people of this region built homes of mud and rock called 'adobe' houses.

Buffalo chasers

407 **The coming of the horse changed life for the Plains people for ever.** Spanish settlers brought horses (and guns!) from Europe. Horses meant that the Native Americans could hunt and kill buffalo much more easily. Buffalo meat became their main food, and they made tents and clothing from buffalo skins.

408 **A successful warrior would become powerful and famous.** But the Plains people thought it was braver to touch an enemy and get away than to simply kill them. This touching was known as 'counting coup'.

409 **The Plains tribes spoke to each other in sign language.** As tribes moved in, they brought different languages. This meant that the best way to put across a message was to use gestures and hand movements.

▼ Buffalo hunters stayed on the move, following the herds across the Plains. They went from camp to camp, where they lived in large tents called tepees. They carried their possessions on a simple horse-drawn trailer called a travois.

FIND OUT YOUR NATIVE AMERICAN NAME

Some Plains people took their names from things which had happened to them. One Sioux woman was called 'The-One-Who-Speaks-Once', and a chief was called 'Young-Man-Afraid-Of-His-Horses'. What do you think you or your friends would be called?

▶ The frame of a tepee was made of poles, arranged in a cone shape. Buffalo skin was stretched over the poles and pegged to the ground. At the top was a hole with a flap which could be opened to let out smoke from the cooking fire inside.

A new world

410 In 1607 about 100 British people, called colonists, landed in what is now Virginia. They founded the first permanent settlement, and others soon followed. The continent was called the New World. Europe was called the Old World.

411 Without help from the Native Americans, the early settlers might have starved. They taught them how to grow new crops such as sweetcorn and potatoes, how to find water and travel by canoe. In return, Europeans brought horses, cattle and metal tools to the New World.

▶ Daniel Boone with his long rifle and hunting dog.

▲ Once the Native Americans learned to trust the newcomers, the two people were able to exchange goods with each other.

412 The earliest white explorers were hunters and trappers. Men like Daniel Boone wandered deep into unknown and unspoilt territory in search of deer and other game. Boone, in particular, loved roaming alone in the wilds of Kentucky. He told his family "Heaven is a Kentucky of a place!"

413 To reach further west, the settlers had somehow to find a route through the Appalachian Mountains. No-one succeeded until 1775, when Daniel Boone led a party through the Cumberland Gap. The track they used became known as the Wilderness Road.

QUIZ

European settlers discovered many sorts of food in America they had never seen before. Which of these are from the Old World, and which from the New?
a) turkey, b) sweetcorn, c) cabbage, d) potatoes, e) beef, f) pasta

a) NW b) NW c) OW d) NW e) OW f) OW

414 The quickest way to reach the wilderness was by river. The giant Mississippi River became a highway for settlers and goods heading for the mid-West from the Gulf of Mexico. They travelled on sailboats or on rafts called flatboats.

▼ Traders float down the Mississippi River on a flatboat. Traders used to carry provisions and equipment up and down the river to trade with the settlers.

Going West

415 **The United States doubled in size in 1803!** The American president, Thomas Jefferson, bought a massive area of land called Louisiana from the French. This was known as the Louisiana Purchase, and included all the land between the Mississippi and the Rocky Mountains.

▲ The Louisiana Purchase, 1803

416 Jefferson sent army officers Meriwether Lewis and William Clark to explore the new territory. They led an expedition up the Missouri River, looking for a route to the Pacific Ocean. After finding a way through the Rockies, they followed the Columbia River down to the sea and became the first people to cross the continent from coast to coast.

417 The National Road was the first highway to the west. Begun in 1811, it ran from Maryland to Illinois and carried a stream of pioneers on horseback or in covered wagons. Towns and other stopping places sprang up along the road.

◄ Pioneers rest from their journey west on the National Road.

418

Native Americans saved Lewis and Clark's lives when they were starving.
Members of the Nez Perce tribe had never seen white people before, but they gave the strangers dried fish and plant roots to eat. They also gave them trees to make canoes so that they could travel downriver more quickly.

I DON'T BELIEVE IT!

Lewis and Clark took with them a Native American guide called Sacagawea. One day, they met a party of fierce Shoshone warriors. By an amazing chance, the Shoshone leader turned out to be Sacagawea's brother!

419

Native Americans were pushed out to make room for white settlers. As Europeans moved west, whole tribes had to move even further west. Among these were the Cherokee tribe who lived in the Southwest. In 1838, soldiers rounded up 15,000 Cherokee and forced them to march to faraway Oklahoma. Over 4,000 of them died on what was called 'The Trail of Tears'.

▲ Cold and starving, the Cherokee are driven away from their ancient homeland and on to a new site west of the Mississippi.

Mountain men

420 The first white people to explore the Rocky Mountains were the trappers. These tough and cunning men spent up to two years alone in the wilds, hunting beavers and other animals for their valuable fur. These 'mountain men' got to know the vast region better than anyone else.

◀ A wild mountain man from the Rockies.

421 The most famous of all the mountain men was Jim Bridger. At the age of 18, he began working as a trapper in the Rockies. He was probably the first white person to see the Great Salt Lake and the wonders of Yellowstone. Bridger spent 40 years in the mountains, and later became a scout for the US Army.

◀ Jim Bridger

422 Many mountain men married Native American wives. They lived lonely and dangerous lives. By marrying, they got company and they also gained family ties with the local tribes.

◀ A white trapper with his wife in a Native American camp in the Rocky Mountains.

423
Mountain men used their skill to guide settlers and explorers. In 1842, Kit Carson led a party along the Oregon Trail and through the Rockies. He even smuggled them safely through a region where the Sioux tribes were hostile. Carson also guided expeditions to California and Utah.

▼ Mountain men have fun at their annual party by the Green River.

424
Every year the trappers met for a big party in the mountains. They gathered in a valley, bringing the loads of furs they had collected to sell and exchange for goods. Then they sang, danced, drank and laughed – and sometimes had fist fights as well. By the end of the party, they were usually penniless again!

Gold rush!

425 In 1848, one of John Sutter's workers found a gold nugget. He was digging on Sutter's farm in California when he saw something shining. "It made my heart thump," he said, "for I was certain it was gold." Then he spotted another piece... and another. He rode off to tell his boss the amazing news.

426 Soon hundreds of gold-seekers were racing to the site. Sutter tried to keep the find a secret, but it leaked out. The famous gold rush had begun. Within months, there were over 4,000 men at work near the river. During 1849 over 80,000 more arrived, walking, riding and by steamship. They were known as the 'Forty-Niners', named after the year of their journey.

▲ The great steam ships of the Mississippi took thousands of prospectors to search for gold.

427 First of all, prospectors had to stake a claim. This means that they chose a piece of land and hammered in a wooden stake to show it was theirs. They might build a simple hut or tent to sleep in, but most of their days were spent hard at work.

428 **The simplest way of looking for gold was 'panning'.** You put some river gravel and water in a metal dish and gently sloshed it about. The lighter pieces were washed out, leaving the gold behind – you hoped!

429 **Most prospectors built a cradle.** This was a large wooden box, which rocked the gravel to separate any gold from the mud and stones. It worked in the same way as with panning.

HOW TO PAN

Find a place where it doesn't matter if you make a mess! Put a scoop of garden soil in a shallow bowl and mix in water until it's sloshy. Now move the bowl in a circle with both hands, letting a little slop over the sides. You'll find the last bits left are the heaviest. If you're lucky they may even be gold!

430 **Towns shot up around the main gold sites.** They were often wild and lawless places, with robberies and fights over rival claims. But few gold rush towns lasted very long. Most miners found no gold at all, and soon gave up their search.

Across the Plains

431 **The cheapest way of reaching the West was by wagon train.** It was also the hardest. The westward trails led over the Plains, which were often deserts with no trees for shelter and no water. There were mountain passes to squeeze through, and deep rivers to cross. And there was always the danger of attacks by Native Americans, angry at people invading their lands.

432 **Most pioneer families travelled in covered wagons.** These were called prairie schooners. A schooner is a type of boat, and the white canvas tops of the prairie schooners looked like sails. The big wheels had broad rims to stop them getting bogged down in mud. The wagons were pulled by teams of horses or oxen.

433 The wagons travelled in a long line.

Dozens of families might join together to form a wagon train. The train would cover about 25 kilometres a day, and only stop at nightfall. Any wagon which broke down was left behind. The travellers had to hurry so that they could cross the mountains before winter snows came.

PICTURE PUZZLE

Can you find the quickest way to get across the Plains and through the mountains? Try to avoid as many dangers as you can.

Barons of beef

434 Texas and the Great Plains were turned into one giant cattle range. As government troops defeated and moved the local tribes, the ranchers came to take their place. They raised huge herds of cattle, guarding them on horseback as they wandered over the open grasslands.

▼ Cowboys drive a herd of cattle over the dry grasslands of Texas.

435 Spaniards brought the first cattle to America in 1521. Over the centuries, these developed into a breed called the Texas Longhorn, which was big and hardy and carried huge pointed horns. Longhorns survived well on the hot dry plains.

► Longhorn cattle were tough, but grew slowly and produced less meat than other breeds.

436

The towns of the East needed the beef of the West. Ranchers began to drive their herds to reach the newly built railroads which would take the animals east. One of the most famous routes was the Chisholm Trail, which ran from Texas to Kansas.

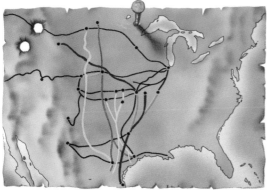

Goodnight–
Loving Trail ——
Western Trail ——
Chisholm Trail ——
Sedalia Trail ——
Shawnee Trail ——
Platcher's Path ——
Nelson Story
Trail ——

▲ These are the most famous of the Wild West cattle trails.

437

Charles Goodnight was a pioneer of the long cattle drives. With his partner Oliver Loving he set out in 1866 to drive 2,000 animals from Texas to Colorado where he sold them. Loving died in a Comanche attack a little later, but the Goodnight-Loving trail lived on.

PICTURE PUZZLE:

Ranchers marked their cattle with their own special brands. Can you match the brand to the name of the ranch?

1.
2.
3. Y
4. Z
5. ⌐

a. Sunrise
b. Rocking 7
c. Bench
d. Hat
e. Hooked Y

1, d; 2, a; 3, e; 4, b; 5, c.

438

Joseph McCoy founded a whole new town – just for cattle. He built huge stockyards to hold cattle in the tiny settlement of Abilene, Kansas. He persuaded the railroad company to lay a new track linking his yard with the main line. Soon the cattle drovers began to make for Abilene as the best place to sell their cattle.

Cowboys at work and play

439 A cowboy had his own special range of equipment. On his head was a wide brimmed hat to keep off sun and rain. He wore leather guards called chaps over his trousers to protect his legs from thorns. Most important of all was a comfortable saddle, where he would sit all day. A cowboy hardly ever carried a gun – it was heavy and got in the way so he usually left it wrapped in his bedroll when on the trail.

Hat

Chaps

440 A cattle drive might last as long as three months. The cowboys worked long days and sometimes into the night. Their job was to keep the cattle together and going the right way. Some rode at the head and others at each side. The worst place was behind the herd, with clouds of dust and flies!

Drag riders

Flank riders

Trail boss

441 At night, the cowboys took turns to keep watch. They rode round the herd, looking for strays. Often, they sang songs to soothe the cattle.

442

A sudden noise might scare the herd and start a stampede, where the cattle race off in a panic. Cowboys tried to stop them by racing in front and waving hats or firing gunshots. This was dangerous work. Their horse might stumble and throw them to the ground where they would be trampled.

443

At the end of the drive was the cow town, where the herd was sold. The cowboys got their pay, put on their best clothes and went out to have fun in the saloons and dance halls. In a day or two their wages would be all gone!

444

Every cowboy carried a rope called a lariat. This had a slip knot so that it could make a loop. Skilled men could catch a cow by throwing the loop over its head or legs.

▶ The lariat was essential for the cowboy to control the cows.

PICTURE PUZZLE:

The chuck wagon carried food for the hungry cowboys. Can you see the bacon, biscuits, beans and coffee that they liked to eat?

Living in a frontier town

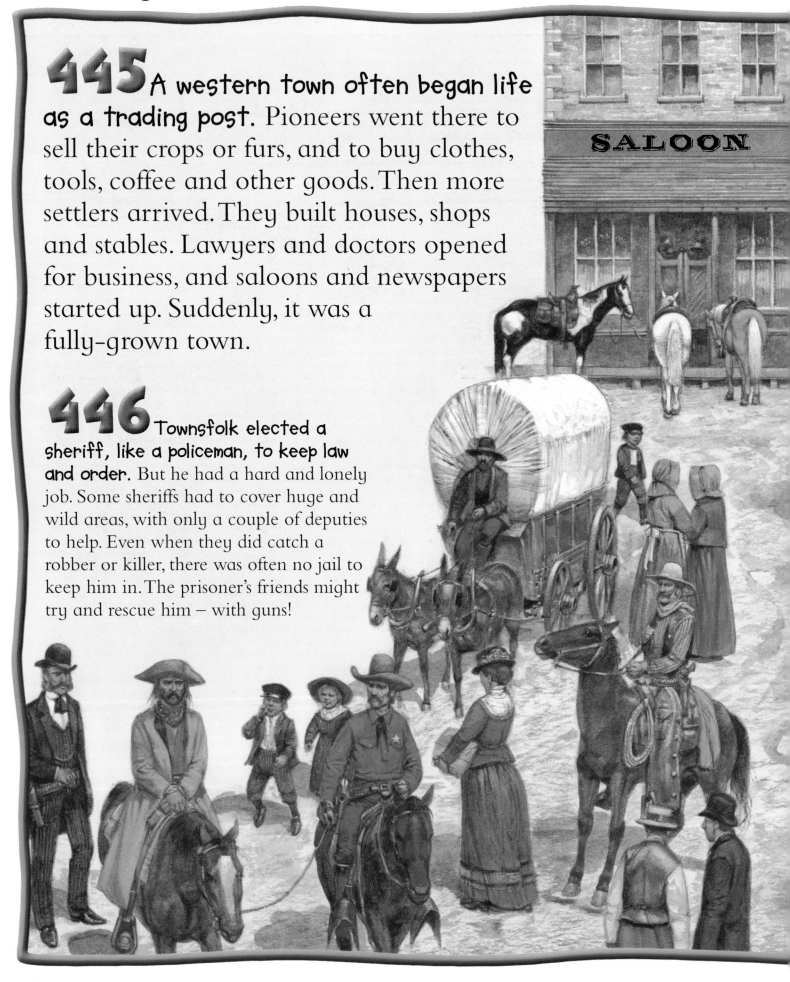

445 **A western town often began life as a trading post.** Pioneers went there to sell their crops or furs, and to buy clothes, tools, coffee and other goods. Then more settlers arrived. They built houses, shops and stables. Lawyers and doctors opened for business, and saloons and newspapers started up. Suddenly, it was a fully-grown town.

446 **Townsfolk elected a sheriff, like a policeman, to keep law and order.** But he had a hard and lonely job. Some sheriffs had to cover huge and wild areas, with only a couple of deputies to help. Even when they did catch a robber or killer, there was often no jail to keep him in. The prisoner's friends might try and rescue him – with guns!

SALOON

447 Cowboys loved drinking, gambling and dancing. They could do all this in the town's saloons. A dancing cowboy made a weird sight, with his huge spurs jingling and his revolvers flapping up and down!

PICTURE PUZZLE:

There were many different kinds of horses in the Wild West. Their names sometimes described their colouring. Can you spot:
an albino (pale-coloured coat)
a pinto (black coat with large white splodges)
a palomino (golden coat and silvery mane and tail)
and an appaloosa (dark, with a white, spotty rump)?

448 Every frontier town had its cheats and con men. The most common of these was the quack doctor or 'pill roller', who sold medicines which he claimed would cure every illness. These miracle drugs were usually made of just chalk or coloured water.

449 One of the most lawless towns was Dodge City in Kansas. So many people were shot that a new cemetery had to be opened in 1872. It was called Boot Hill, because gunmen were buried there still wearing their boots.

Getting around

450 **For most people, the easiest way to travel was by stagecoach.** There were coaches linking most big towns. One company ran four coaches a week between St Louis and San Francisco. They kept moving day and night, covering about 160 kilometres in 24 hours. But the journey was not much fun. The roads were bumpy and bad, and passengers ended the trip bruised and dusty.

Guard

Passengers

Broad wheels to avoid the stagecoach sinking into the ground.

451 **Stagecoaches were far safer than travelling alone.** Bandits or Native Americans often attacked travellers in remote places. A group of well-armed passengers could defend themselves better than a lone horseman.

Here are how the letters look in Morse Code. The dashes are the long buzzes, and the dots the short ones. You can use Morse to send secret messages to a friend – as long as they've got this book too!

A ●—	J ●———	S ●●●
B —●●●	K —●—	T —
C —●—●	L ●—●●	U ●●—
D —●●	M ——	V ●●●—
E ●	N —●	W ●——
F ●●—●	O ———	X —●●—
G ——●	P ●——●	Y —●——
H ●●●●	Q ——●—	Z ——●●
I ●●	R ●—●	

452

The quickest way to send mail was by pony express. A rider set off with his postbag riding as fast as he could, and changing to a fresh pony every 20 kilometres. After about 120 kilometres, he handed on his mail to the next rider. In this way, letters could be carried up to 320 kilometres in a day.

▲ Stagecoaches were usually pulled by two or four horses.

453

The most famous stagecoach company was Wells Fargo. Its coaches carried passengers, goods and mail from New York to the far West. Wells Fargo wagons also took gold and silver from western mines back to the East.

454

By the 1860s, most towns were linked by the telegraph. Messages could be sent over huge distances along wires. They were turned into Morse Code (a system of long and short buzzes) which the operator tapped out.

The iron horse

455 During the 1860s, railroads were laid into the Wild West. The government saw that railroads would attract more settlers. Soon two companies started laying new tracks – one from the East and one from the West. They would join up to form the first railroad right across North America.

▲ The railroads built in America up to 1900.

456 Building a railroad across the Rockies was very difficult. Thousands of men had to hack and blast away rock to make cuttings and build huge bridges to make the track as level as possible. They had to cope with fierce heat, and snow. There were also many raids by Native Americans, who were angry at the arrival of what they called 'the iron horse'.

457 In 1869, the two railroads that were running across America met in the state of Utah. The rival companies raced each other over the final stretch, each laying up to 16 kilometres of line a day. Telegraph wires ran alongside the line to send back news of each day's total.

458 Over 11,000 Chinese workers helped to build the Central Pacific Railroad. They were tougher and more efficient than the white workers, partly because they ate more healthy food. They never drank liquor or smoked, and rarely went on strike.

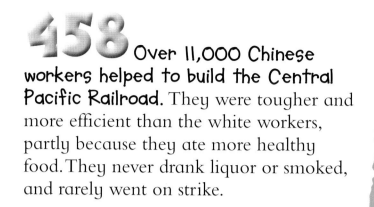

◄ Chinese labourers lay wooden sleepers and metal rails through the wilderness.

459 Train travel was faster and more comfortable than going by stagecoach. There were still dangers though. Trains might get stuck in snowdrifts, or be rocked by winds howling across the Plains. Outlaws could easily halt a train by taking out rails or blocking the track with logs. When it stopped, they climbed on board and robbed the passengers or freight cars.

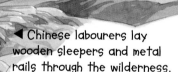

◄ Pulled by steam power, people could travel faster than a galloping horse.

Buffalo shoot

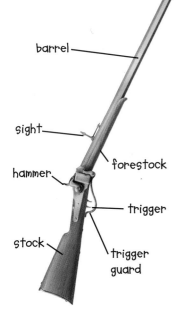

barrel

sight

hammer

forestock

trigger

stock

trigger guard

460 Millions of buffalo roamed the Plains. They seemed to be an ideal source of food for the armies of railroad builders. So sharpshooters were hired to kill buffalo every day. A new kind of rifle was invented which could hit a buffalo at over 500 metres. "It shoots today and kills tomorrow," one hunter said.

461 The most famous of buffalo killers was Buffalo Bill. Born William Cody, he worked as a scout and cowhand before joining the railroad. He was an amazing shot, bringing down a buffalo with almost every bullet. In a year and a half, he killed over 4,000 animals.

462 The native Americans were angry at the slaughter. The buffalo was a sacred animal to them, and vital to their way of life. In 1874, the Cheyenne and other tribes attacked the white hunters and drove them away. But army troops soon took revenge, defeating all the people of the southern Plains and forcing them onto special areas called reservations.

463 Buffalo hunting soon became a sport. Men came from all over the USA to join in the killing. Thousands of beasts were shot every day. By the 1880s the great herds had almost disappeared from the Plains.

464 At the end of the 19th century, the American buffalo was almost extinct. So many had been killed that there were nearly none left. Then at last it became a protected species which could not be hunted. Today there are many buffalo living on specially fenced game reserves, as well as wild herds in some national parks.

I DON'T BELIEVE IT!

Buffalo hunting became such a famous sport that a Grand Duke came all the way from Russia for it. He missed, at point blank range, with his first 12 shots!

Custer's last stand

465 The tribes of the Plains fought to keep their traditional hunting grounds. There were many battles between gold miners and the Cheyenne in Colorado. But the Cheyenne leader, Black Kettle, wanted peace. He took his people to a meeting with the army at Sand Creek in 1864. But the US troops attacked Black Kettle's camp and killed the people, mostly women and children.

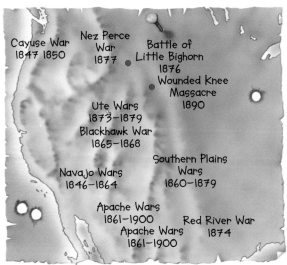

Cayuse War 1847 1850
Nez Perce War 1877
Battle of Little Bighorn 1876
Wounded Knee Massacre 1890
Ute Wars 1873–1879
Blackhawk War 1865–1868
Southern Plains Wars 1860–1879
Navajo Wars 1846–1864
Apache Wars 1861–1900
Apache Wars 1861–1900
Red River War 1874

▲ This map shows the areas of warfare in the West between settlers and Native Americans.

466 The US government had promised to let the Sioux live undisturbed in the Black Hills of Dakota. But in 1871 workers began building a railroad through the hills. In 1874 a gold rush brought thousands of miners into the area. The promise was forgotten.

◀ A Sioux chief in traditional dress.

▲ Red Cloud, a chief of the Lakota tribes of the Sioux.

467 The American government offered to buy the Black Hills. Spotted Tail, a Sioux chief, demanded $70 million. Red Cloud, another chief, asked for enough meat to feed the tribe for 200 years! But Little Big Man wanted war. "I will kill the first chief who speaks for selling the Black Hills!" he shouted.

468 Three long columns of soldiers rode into Dakota in 1876. Their job was to move the Sioux off their ancient hunting grounds. The troops were led by General George Crook, who had just defeated the Apache people in the south. Also in the force was George Custer, known by the Sioux as 'Hard Backsides', because he would chase them all day without leaving his saddle.

WORD PUZZLE

Unscramble the words to make up the names of 5 great Native American leaders:

CLOUDKETTLE
BULLCRAZYTAILBLACK
SITTINGREDHORSESPOTTED

a) Sitting Bull b) Crazy Horse c) Black Kettle d) Spotted Tail e) Red Cloud

469 Custer believed that he alone would destroy the Sioux. That June he led his men towards the Little Bighorn River. He was in for a shock. His force met a Sioux and Cheyenne war party led by Crazy Horse, which surrounded it and killed every single man. It was the greatest of all the Native American victories – but it was also one of the last.

Outlaws and lawmen

470 Abilene was a cow town, full of wild cowboys who were hard to control. In 1871 a new marshal arrived – James 'Wild Bill' Hickok. He was tall and carried a pair of ivory-handled pistols in his belt. The townsfolk were terrified. Wild Bill was said to have killed ten men, and he looked, one said, "like a mad old bull". But for a few months he brought peace to Abilene.

471 Wyatt Earp tamed the gunmen of Dodge City with his long-barrelled 'Buntline Special' revolver. When one famous killer rode into town looking for trouble he found Earp standing at the saloon door. He was halfway through drawing his gun when he felt the lawman's Special in his ribs. "Reckon I'll be going", he said. "Go ahead," said Earp, "and don't come back!"

▲ The cabin tucked away in the Wyoming Hills where Butch Cassidy and other gang members hid out.

▲ This is a Smith and Wesson .44 revolver, favoured by many of the gunslingers of the Wild West.

472 Butch Cassidy and the Sundance Kid were two of the best-known outlaws. They robbed banks, held up trains and stole cattle. With marshals on their trail, they hid in a remote part of Wyoming called the Hole-in-the-Wall country. With other thieves, they became known as the 'Hole-in-the-Wall' Gang.

473 The James Gang brought terror to the Wild West. Brothers Jesse and Frank James were brutal thugs, who often beat up or killed their victims before robbing them. In 1882 one of the gang shot Jesse in the back of the head so that he could claim the reward money.

474 Belle Starr was known as 'The Bandit Queen'. She ran a gang in Texas which stole horses and cattle, then married a notorious rustler. Next came a spell in jail. Even when her husband was shot dead in a saloon gunfight, she carried on with her criminal career. Belle was gunned down in an ambush in 1889.

475 Judge Roy Bean was the only lawman for 400 miles in outlaw country west of the Pecos mountains. He ran his court from the bar of his own saloon, selling beer while he handed out instant penalties to rustlers and killers. He usually sentenced them to be hanged.

Rustlers and sharpshooters

476 Cattle and horses were easy to steal. The people that stole them were called rustlers. The herds roamed over the prairie, and could not be guarded all the time. A band of rustlers could simply ride up to the animals and drive them away. They took them to a hideout, or 'shebang', and changed their brand markings.

477 Ranchers formed groups to deal with the rustlers. One of the most famous groups was called Stuart's Stranglers. Led by Granville Stuart, the Stranglers tracked down rustlers throughout Montana and then hanged them. Stuart always fixed a note to each body, saying 'Horse Thief' or 'Cattle Thief'.

WANTED
HORSE THIEF
BILL HICKS

WANTED
CATTLE THIEF
JOHN CLINTON

▲ Posters were put up to try to catch the rustlers. The penalty if you were caught was usually death.

478 There were many feuds (quarrels) between the farmers. Big ranchers were angry when new settlers arrived and fenced off parts of the prairie for their stock animals. Sometimes, these feuds led to what were called range wars. The rival ranchers hired armies of gunmen to fight for them.

479 Billy the Kid was one of the most famous outlaws of the Wild West. His real name may have been Henry McCarty, and he fought in a range war in New Mexico. In 1881 he was cornered and shot by Sheriff Pat Garrett. According to legend, Billy killed 27 men – the real total was probably just 4!

480 Disaster struck the cattle ranchers in the winter of 1886–1887. Blizzards swept across the prairies, and snow and ice covered the grass. Hundreds of thousands of cattle died. One cowboy recalled "the first day I rode out, I never saw a live animal".

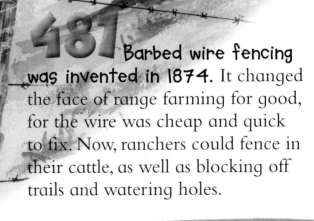

481 Barbed wire fencing was invented in 1874. It changed the face of range farming for good, for the wire was cheap and quick to fix. Now, ranchers could fence in their cattle, as well as blocking off trails and watering holes.

Homesteaders

482 **The Homestead Act of 1862 brought a flood of new settlers to the Plains.** Under the new law, anyone who paid $10 could claim 160 acres of farmland, as long as they stayed five years. Thousands of people came from the East to set up their own homesteads.

483 **Life was hard for the homesteader.** Water was scarce on the plains, so first of all he had to dig a well. Then he had to plough his patch of grassland with oxen and raise crops. But these could be ruined by droughts, prairie fires and storms, or by plagues of grasshoppers. If food got short in the harsh winter, he might have to kill and eat his faithful oxen.

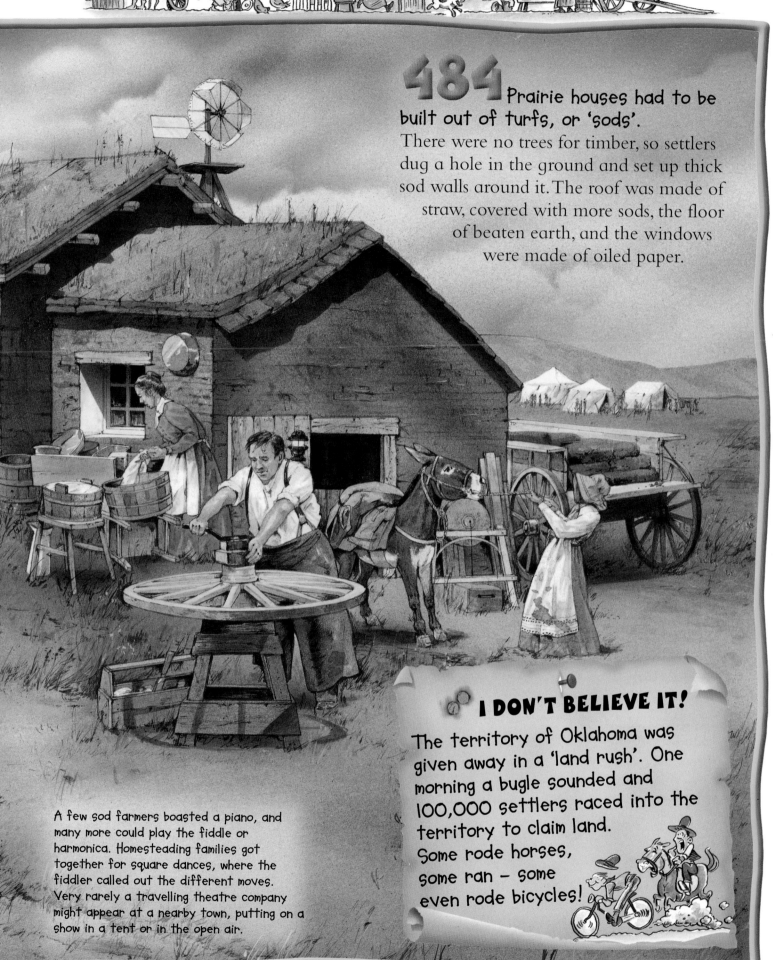

484 Prairie houses had to be built out of turfs, or 'sods'.

There were no trees for timber, so settlers dug a hole in the ground and set up thick sod walls around it. The roof was made of straw, covered with more sods, the floor of beaten earth, and the windows were made of oiled paper.

A few sod farmers boasted a piano, and many more could play the fiddle or harmonica. Homesteading families got together for square dances, where the fiddler called out the different moves. Very rarely a travelling theatre company might appear at a nearby town, putting on a show in a tent or in the open air.

I DON'T BELIEVE IT!

The territory of Oklahoma was given away in a 'land rush'. One morning a bugle sounded and 100,000 settlers raced into the territory to claim land. Some rode horses, some ran – some even rode bicycles!

Disappearing tribes

485 By the 1880s, most Native Americans in the USA had been moved onto reservations in the West. These were mostly on poor farm land, with no game to hunt. The tribes depended on the government to hand out food, clothing and medicines. Many died of disease or starvation.

▼ This map shows the main reservations where Native Americans were forced to live.

486 Many of the Sioux tribes refused to go to the reservations. After their victory at the Little Bighorn, a band led by Sitting Bull had fled across the northern borders and into Canada. This country was ruled by the British, who let the newcomers live freely. US troops did not dare go in and capture Sitting Bull.

▼ Traditional costume was a source of great pride to Native Americans.

▼ Dressed in white people's clothes they felt humiliated.

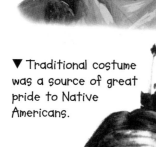

487 Social workers and clergymen tried to change the Native Americans' way of life. They thought they should forget their old traditions and copy white customs – wear European clothes, speak English, go to school and give up their traditional tribal religions. This made many Native Americans very unhappy.

488 The Nez Perce people lived in the beautiful Wallowa Valley in Oregon. Led by Chief Joseph, they refused to move to a reservation. When soldiers came to drive them out in 1877, they decided to take refuge in faraway Canada. Chief Joseph started an amazing journey. With 800 men, women and children he dodged all the troops sent to capture him. They trekked over 1,600 kilometres before resting short of the Canadian border. But here the soldiers caught up with them. Chief Joseph surrendered, saying "I will fight no more forever."

489 The government sent the Nez Perce to a marshy reservation in Oklahoma. Without their mountain air and water, a quarter of the people became sick and died. Chief Joseph never went home again. He died in 1904 – some said of a broken heart.

◀ Chief Joseph

QUIZ

1. In what year was barbed wire invented?
2. How much did 160 acres of land cost in 1862?
3. Which country ruled Canada at this time?
4. When did Chief Joseph die?

1. 1874; 2. $10; 3. Britain; 4. 1904.

490 The Sioux leader Crazy Horse surrendered to white soldiers in 1877. He led his people out of the Black Hills and onto the reservation. The procession of warriors, women, children and ponies stretched for more than three km behind him. A few months later, Crazy Horse was arrested. When he tried to escape, he was stabbed to death.

Massacre at Wounded Knee

491 The Native Americans had all been locked up in their reservations. They seemed to have no more power. But in 1889 they suddenly got new hope. A Paiute leader called Wovoka dreamed that the settlers could be defeated. To do this, the people must perform a 'Ghost Dance', and wear Ghost Shirts which would protect them from the bullets of the enemy.

492 The Sioux began dancing the Ghost Dance. Sitting Bull had by now returned from Canada, and joined the movement. This alarmed the US army, who sent soldiers to arrest him. There was a fight, and Sitting Bull – the greatest of Sioux leaders - was shot dead.

493 The Apache people had been forced to live in a hot dry area of Arizona. Many hated it, and ran away to the mountains of Mexico. Leaders such as Geronimo lived by making raids on cattle herds and small settlements, and soon a force of troops was sent after them. There was a long chase, but in the end the Apaches surrendered.

◀ Geronimo, one of the last great rebels against white rule.

494 Two years later, an Apache band escaped again. Led by Geronimo, they hid in the harsh 'badlands' of New Mexico, but soldiers caught up with them. Once more Geronimo disappeared with a handful of followers. He had by now become a public hero, and after he finally surrendered in 1886 he remained a celebrity.

SITTING BULL'S SONG

Here is the sad song of Sitting Bull after his surrender.

A warrior	I-ki-ci-ze
I have been	wa-on kon
Now	he wa-na he
It is all over.	na-la ye-lo
A hard time	he i-yo-ti-ye
I have.	ki-yawa-on

495 Big Foot was the last of the great Sioux chiefs. But he had only about 350 followers, mostly women and children. In 1890 the army ordered them to march to Wounded Knee Creek. An argument started, and the soldiers opened fire with their powerful guns. Within a few minutes, about 250 of the Sioux people lay dead. Later on the dead were buried in a big pit.

▶ Big Foot lay frozen on the ground after he was shot dead at Wounded Knee.

The end of the Wild West

496 Buffalo Bill gave up his job as a buffalo hunter and army scout and became an entertainer instead. In 1883 he formed his 'Wild West Show', which toured the world for many years. Thrilled audiences could see buffalo, real cowboys, trick shooting and horseriding, stagecoaches and mock battles with Native Americans. Sitting Bull even appeared in the show for a short time!

▲ Some of the cowboy tricks in Buffalo Bill's show were riding a bucking bronco, rope tricks and throwing a lasso as well as sharp shooting by Annie Oakley.

497 Annie Oakley was an amazing sharpshooter. She learned to shoot when she was just eight years old, and went on to star in Buffalo Bill's Wild West Show. In her act she shot cigarettes out of her husband's mouth, and hit a playing card tossed into the air. Sitting Bull called her 'Little Sure Shot'.

I DON'T BELIEVE IT!

In the early 1900s even Geronimo became a tourist attraction. He charged visitors money to take photographs of him. One picture shows him at the wheel of a car – even though he couldn't drive!

498 The government wanted Native Americans to become farmers. But land on the reservations was often poor, and few were interested in raising crops. Instead, many sold their plots of land and lived off the money. When that ran out, they had nothing.

499 The Wild West vanished long ago. The legends live on, in books, TV dramas and films. In fact many of the first motion pictures were set in the west, and 'westerns' have been made ever since. But the world shown on the big screen is a long way from the real thing – no cowboy ever fired so accurately as John Wayne!

500 In 1872 Yellowstone became the first national park in the world. This beautiful wild region contained lakes, waterfalls, mountains and forests. By the end of the 1800s, thousands of tourists were flocking to Yellowstone every year. In 1913, cars were allowed into the park for the first time. Visitors could now experience the landscape of the Wild West.

Let's have some fun!

EGYPT WORD SEARCH

There are nine words to do with Ancient Egypt are hidden in this letter square. Can you find them all?

N	P	E	P	I	C	X	M
A	Y	H	K	L	D	C	U
D	R	W	A	T	E	N	M
C	A	I	P	R	T	W	M
M	M	G	B	A	A	G	Y
N	I	L	E	L	M	O	N
D	D	Y	S	O	R	C	H

Pepi, pharaoh, pyramid, Ra (sun god), wig, Nile, Bes (dwarf god), mummy, Aten (new sun god)

QUIZ

1. How many gates were there into the city of Rome?
2. What did the Romans call Valentine's Day?
3. How many stages were there in a Roman bath?
4. Which English queen fought the Romans?
5. Who was king of the Roman gods?

1. 37 gates 2. Lupercalia 3. Five 4. Boudicca 5. Jupiter

MAKE YOUR OWN TEPEE!

You can make your very own tepee in your back garden, and be like Geronimo or Sitting Bull!
First, ask an adult from some long garden canes. Ask them to help you push one end of each into the ground in a circle. Make sure that the canes are leaning towards each other, as next you want to tie the tops together with string. Now ask for an old blanket. Wrap the blanket round the outside of the frame and tie it at the top. Leave a space to get in, and you're ready to prowl the prairie!

Quiz

1. How long did it take to become a knight?
2. What was the system of using coats of arms called?
3. What was a troubadour?
4. What is the name of the tapestry that records the Battle of Hastings in 1066?
5. Who was the Muslim leader that fought the knights of the Third Crusade?

1. 14 years 2. Heraldry 3. A poet-musician who composed songs about love 4. the Bayeaux Tapestry 5. Saladin

What doesn't belong?

Can you find the objects in these two pictures that shouldn't be there? Can you see a cowboy hat on an Egyptian? Or an Egyptian crown on a pirate? What else can you find?

Index